knitting over the edge

unique ribs • cords • appliqués • colors • nouveau

knitting over the edge

unique ribs • cords • appliqués • colors • nouveau

the second essential collection of decorative borders

nicky epstein

author of *Knitting on the Edge*

sixth&spring books

To Madame Defarge—A rotten person...but a dedicated knitter!

sixth&spring
books

Editorial Director
TRISHA MALCOLM

Art Director
CHI LING MOY

Book Manager
ERICA SMITH

Executive Editor
CARLA SCOTT

Instructions Editors
LOUISA CAMERON-SMITH
SANDI PROSSER
CHARLOTTE QUIGGLE

Instructions Proofreader
MARY LOU EASTMAN

Technical Illustrations
ULI MÖNCH

Graphic Designer
MATT DOJNY

Production Manager
DAVID JOINNIDES

Photography
JACK DEUTSCH STUDIOS

President, Sixth&Spring Books
ART JOINNIDES

Library of Congress Control Number: 2005923949

ISBN 1-931543-75-5

Manufactured in China

1 3 5 7 9 10 8 6 4 2

First Edition

contents

introduction

My inspiration for this book came by way of the great success of, and reader enthusiasm for, my *Knitting on the Edge* book. The worldwide response was overwhelming. With the encouragement of my editor, Trisha Malcolm—the wind beneath my wings— I dove once again into the world of edgings.

The work was intense but gratifying, and I am happy to share this completely new and comprehensive collection with knitters of all skills.

These patterns may look complex—but do not be intimidated! When you try them, you will be amazed at how easy they are to make and how much they will enhance your knitted pieces. Experiment with them, use them creatively, and enjoy!

You will find an exciting variety of extraordinary edgings and techniques, including cords, appliqués, and color work—many of which I have created for this book. I've also included five of my original designs, one to open each chapter.

The tradition of knitting was passed on to me by my mother and grandmother, and I hope this book perpetuates that tradition and encourages you to knit, to learn, and to pass along your love of knitting to others.

If you've been knitting on the edge I cordially invite you to start knitting *over* the edge. It's a lot of fun!

Happy knitting,

Nicky Epstein

textures and size

The following "circles" edgings illustrate the difference yarn texture and size can make in how an edging looks. I used a variety of yarns of different weights and textures along with corresponding needle sizes for each yarn. The circles are made using the original instructions (see pg. 84) with a 4" (10cm) long cord. The space between the cord varies. I used 4" (10cm) cord length for all the swatches in order to illustrate the effect the size of the yarn has on the space between the circles. If you would like the circles to be spaced more closely or further apart, you will have to make the cord length shorter or longer by changing row amounts or the stitch amounts between each circle.

5

1 alpaca

2 angora

3 cotton

4 ribbon

5 bouclé

6 fur blend

7 chenille

6

7

8 fleece

9 linen

10 mohair

notes on using this book

Directional Symbols

There are several ways to create edgings: knitting from the bottom up, knitting from the top down, or knitting separately, then turning the edging horizontally in order to pick up stitches along the selvage edge or sewing onto the main piece. In most of the instructions, we have used the symbols shown below to indicate the direction in which the edging was knit. In many cases, the edgings in this book are reversible.

▲ Knit from bottom up: Cast-on edge is the lower edge.

▼ Knit from the top down: Bound-off edge is the lower edge.

▶ Knit separately: Stitches can be picked up or sewn on.

◀▶ Reversible: Both sides are the same or equally attractive.

▶▲ Knit separately: stitches are joined together onto one needle, sometimes adding stitches in between, then the edging continues upward.

▼▶▲ The center is worked separately, then encased by picking up stitches along bottom and top and working in either direction.

Standard Yarn Weights

In the Patterns chapter, next to the suggested yarn in the Materials section, we have used the Standard Yarn Weight System for ease in substitution. If you plan to substitute a yarn, be sure to knit a gauge swatch and check that it matches the original gauge in the pattern and has a similar appearance to the original yarn used in the pattern. These standard yarn weights can be used for any pattern.

Making Cords

When making cords, use two double-pointed needles or one short circular needle, unless otherwise indicated. The cords are made separately, then either sewn on or knit into the piece to form the edging. If you sew on the cord, use a tapestry needle and the same yarn used to make the cord. Pin the cord in place on top of the fabric. Use small running stitches, work from the wrong side, catching the cord with each stitch.

For terms and abbreviations used in this book, see page 188.

Standard Yarn Weight System

Categories of yarn, gauge ranges, and recommended needle and hook sizes

Yarn Weight Symbol & Category Names	1 Super Fine	2 Fine	3 Light	4 Medium	5 Bulky	6 Super Bulky
Type of Yarns in Category	Sock, Fingering, Baby	Sport, Baby	DK, Light Worsted	Worsted, Afghan, Aran	Chunky, Craft, Rug	Bulky, Roving
Knit Gauge Range* in Stockinette Stitch to 4 Inches	27–32 sts	23–26 sts	21–24 sts	16–20 sts	12–15 sts	6–11 sts
Recommended Needle in Metric Size Range	2.25–3.25 mm	3.25–3.75 mm	3.75–4.5 mm	4.5–5.5 mm	5.5–8 mm	8 mm and larger
Recommended Needle U.S. Size Range	1 to 3	3 to 5	5 to 7	7 to 9	9 to 11	11 and larger

*Guidelines only: The above reflect the most commonly used gauges and needle sizes for specific yarn categories.

unique

ribs

looped rib I

▲ (multiple of 4 sts plus 3)

• Loops may also be cut for fringe look.

Make loop (ML) Wyib, insert RH needle knitwise into st, wind yarn clockwise around RH needle and first 2 fingers of left hand twice, then over RH needle point once more, draw all 3 loops through st and place them on LH needle, then k the loops and original st tog tbl.

Rows 1 and 3 (RS) *K1, p1; rep from *, end k1.

Row 2 *P1, k1; rep from *, end p1.

Row 4 *P1, k1, p1, ML; rep from *, end p1, k1, p1.

Rep rows 1 to 4 once more, then rep rows 1 and 2 until desired length.

Cont as desired.

looped rib II

▲ (odd number of sts)

• Make loop (ML) as for Looped Rib I.

Row 1 (RS) *K1, p1; rep from *, end k1.

Row 2 *P1, ML; rep from *, end p1.

Row 3 Rep row 1.

Row 4 *P1, k1; rep from *, end p1.

Rep rows 3 and 4 until desired length.

Cont as desired.

ribs

fringed rib

▲ (multiple of 4 sts plus 3)

Make tassel (MT) Wyib, insert RH needle knitwise into st, wind yarn clockwise around RH needle and first 3 fingers of left hand 5 times, then over RH needle point once more, draw all 6 loops through st and place them on LH needle, then k the loops and original st tog tbl.

Row 1 (RS) *K1, p1; rep from *, end k1.

Row 2 P1, *MT, p1, k1, p1; rep from *, end MT, p1.

Row 3 Rep row 1.

Row 4 *P1, k1; rep from *, end p1.

Rep rows 3 and 4 until desired length.

Cont as desired.

Cut loops and trim evenly.

wrapped tassel 2 x 3 rib

▲ (multiple of 5 sts plus 2)

• Make tassel (MT) as for Fringed Rib.

Wrap 3 (W3) Wyif sl next 3 sts purlwise, pass yarn to back, sl same 3 sts back to LH needle, pass yarn to front, sl sts back to RH needle, pass yarn to back.

Row 1 (WS) *P2, k3; rep from *, end p2.

Row 2 *K2, p3; rep from *, end k2.

Row 3 *P2, k1, MT, k1; rep from *, end p2.

Row 4 *K2, W3; rep from *, end k2.

Rep rows 1 and 2 until desired length.

Cont as desired.

Cut loops and trim evenly.

wrapped tassel 3 x 3 rib

▲ (multiple of 6 sts plus 3)

• Make tassel (MT) as for Fringed Rib.

Row 1 (RS) *K3, p3; rep from *, end k3.

Row 2 *P1, MT, p1, k3; rep from *, end p1, MT, p1.

Row 3 Rep row 1.

Row 4 *P3, k3; rep from *, end p3.

Rep rows 3 and 4 until desired length.

Cont as desired.

Cut loops and trim evenly.

top tassel 1 x 1 rib

▲ (multiple of 4 sts plus 1)

• Make tassel (MT) as for Fringed Rib.

Row 1 (RS) *P1, k1; rep from *, end p1.

Row 2 *K1, p1; rep from *, end k1.

Rep rows 1 and 2 until desired length, end with row 1.

Next row (WS) K1, p1, *MT, p1, k1, p1; rep from *, end MT, p1, k1.

Cont as desired.

ribs

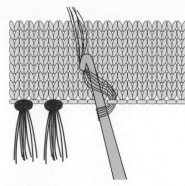

Simple Fringe

Cut yarn twice desired length plus extra for knotting. On wrong side, insert hook from front to back through piece and over folded yarn. Pull yarn through. Draw ends through and tighten. Trim yarn.

1 x 1 bobble rib/fringe

▲ (multiple of 4 sts plus 3)

Make bobble (MB) [(P1, k1) twice, p1] into same st—5 sts; pass 2nd, 3rd, 4th and 5th sts, one at a time, over first st.

Row 1 (RS) *P1, k1, p1, MB; rep from *, end p1, k1, p1.

Row 2 *K1, p1; rep from *, end k1.

Row 3 *P1, k1; rep from *, end p1.

Row 4 Rep row 2.

Rep rows 3 and 4 until desired length.

Cont as desired.

With crochet hook, attach fringe along lower edge, with each fringe section centered under a bobble.

double seed st with bobbles/fringe

▲ (multiple of 4 sts plus 1)

Make bobble (MB) K into front, back, front, back and front of same st—5 sts; [turn, k5, turn, p5] twice; pass 2nd, 3rd, 4th, and 5th sts, one at a time, over first st.

Row 1 (RS) Purl.

Row 2 Knit.

Rows 3, 6, 10 and 11 K1, *p1, k1; rep from * to end.

Rows 4, 5, 8 and 9 P1, *k1, p1; rep from * to end.

Row 7 K1, *p1, MB, p1, k1; rep from * to end.

Row 12 Purl.

Rows 13 and 14 Knit.

With RS facing and crochet hook, pull a loop of 3-strand fringe through a st just under a bobble, leaving ends of fringe on RS of work; pull ends through loop. If desired, braid fringe.

1 x 1 rib/unraveled fringe

▶ (over 11 sts)

Row 1 (RS) [K1, p1] 3 times, k5.

Row 2 P5, [k1, p1] 3 times.

Rep rows 1 and 2 until desired length.

Next row (RS) Bind off 7 sts, cut yarn and tie off rem st on RH needle, sl rem sts off needle and unravel them down to first row.

Cut ends of loops and trim evenly.

seeded rib/unraveled fringe

▶ (over 17 sts)

Row 1 (RS) [K3, p3] twice, k5.

Row 2 P5, [k1, p1] 6 times.

Rep rows 1 and 2 until desired length.

Next row (RS) Bind off 12 sts, cut yarn and tie off rem st on RH needle. Sl rem sts off needle and unravel them down to first row. Cut ends of loops and trim evenly.

ribs

rick rack rib/unraveled fringe

▶ (over 17 sts)

Row 1 (RS) K5, [p2, k2] 3 times.

Row 2 [P2, k2] 3 times, p5.

Row 3 K6, [p2, k2] twice, p2, k1.

Row 4 P1, [k2, p2] 3 times, p4.

Row 5 K7, [p2, k2] twice, p2.

Row 6 [K2, p2] 3 times, p5.

Row 7 K5, p1, [k2, p2] twice, k2, p1.

Row 8 K1, [p2, k2] twice, p2, k1, p5.

Rows 9 and 10 Rep rows 1 and 2.

Rows 11 and 12 Rep rows 7 and 8.

Rows 13 and 14 Rep rows 5 and 6.

Rows 15 and 16 Rep rows 3 and 4.

Rep rows 1 to 16 until desired length, end with row 1.

Next row (WS) Bind off 12 sts in pat, cut yarn and tie off rem st on RH needle. Sl rem sts off needle and unravel them down to first row. Cut ends of loops and trim evenly.

baby cable rib/unraveled fringe

▶ (over 19 sts)

1/1 RT K2tog, leaving sts on needle, then k first st again; sl both sts off needle.

Row 1 (RS) [P2, k2] 3 times, p1, k6.

Rows 2 and 4 P6, k1, [p2, k2] 3 times.

Row 3 [P2, 1/1 RT] 3 times, p1, k6.

Rep rows 1 to 4 until desired length.

Next row (RS) Bind off 12 sts, cut yarn and tie off rem sts on RH needle, sl rem sts off needle and unravel them down to first row. Cut ends of loops and trim evenly.

short 'n long garter rib/unraveled fringe

▶ (over 16 sts)

Row 1 (RS) K2, p2, k3, p2, k7.

Rows 2 and 4 Purl.

Row 3 K2, p7, k7.

Rep rows 1 to 4 until desired length.

Next row (RS) Bind off 10 sts, cut yarn and tie off rem sts on RH needle. Sl rem sts off needle and unravel them down to first row. Cut ends of loops and trim evenly.

rib check/unraveled loops

▶ (over 16 sts)

Rows 1, 3 and 5 (RS) K3, p2, k2, p2, k7.

Rows 2, 4 and 6 P7, [k2, p2] twice, p1.

Rows 7, 9 and 11 K1, [p2, k2] twice, p2, k5.

Rows 8, 10 and 12 P5, [k2, p2] twice, k2, p1.

Rep rows 1 to 12 until desired length, end with row 6.

Next row (RS) Bind off 11 sts, cut yarn and tie off rem sts on RH needle. Sl rem sts off needle and unravel them down to first row.

basketweave rib/ unraveled tassel fringe

▶ (over 24 sts)

Row 1 (RS) Knit.

Rows 2 and 4 K4, p3, k5, p3, k4, p5.

Row 3 K5, p4, k3, p5, k3, p4.

Row 5 Knit.

Rows 6 and 8 [P3, k5] twice, p8.

Row 7 K8, [p5, k3] twice.

Rep rows 1 to 8 until desired length.

Next row (RS) K5, bind off rem sts. Slip 5 sts off needle and unravel them down to first row. Cut ends of loops to create fringe. *Knot 4 strands of fringe tog, with knot as close to edging as possible; rep from * along entire edging. Trim fringe ends evenly.

basketweave rib reversed

welted rib/unraveled loops

▶ (over 16 sts)

Row 1 (RS) K6, p5, k5.

Row 2 P5, k5, p6.

Row 3 Knit.

Row 4 P10, k5, p1.

Row 5 K1, p5, k10.

Row 6 Purl.

Rep rows 1 to 6 until desired length, end with row 2.

Next row (RS) Bind off 11 sts, cut yarn and tie off rem sts on RH needle. Sl rem sts off needle and unravel them down to first row.

1 x 1 bobble rib/unraveled fringe

▶ (over 15 sts)

Make bobble (MB) K into front, back, front, back and front of same st—5 sts; turn, p5, turn, k5, pass 2nd, 3rd, 4th, and 5th sts, one at a time, over first st.

Rows 1 and 3 (RS) K6, [p1, k1] 4 times, p1.

Rows 2, 4 and 6 [K1, p1] 4 times, k1, p6.

Row 5 K6, p1, k1, p1, MB, [p1, k1] twice, p1.

Rep rows 1 to 6 until desired length, end with row 3.

Next row (WS) Bind off 8 sts, cut yarn and tie off rem sts on RH needle.

Sl rem sts off needle and unravel them down to first row. Cut ends of loops and trim evenly.

flower and stem pat/unraveled loops

▶ (over 17 sts)

1/1 RC Sl 1 st to cn and hold to back, k1, k1 from cn.

1/1 LC Sl 1 st to cn and hold to front, k1, k1 from cn.

1/1 RPC Sl 1 st to cn and hold to back, k1, p1 from cn.

1/1 LPC Sl 1 st to cn and hold to front, p1, k1 from cn.

Row 1 (WS) K5, p1, k1, p2, k2, p1, k5.

Row 2 P5, 1/1 LPC, p1, 1/1 LPC, 1/1 RPC, p5.

Row 3 K6, p2, k2, p1, k6.

Row 4 P4, [k1, yo, k1] into next st, turn and p3, turn and [k1, yo twice] 3 times, p1, 1/1 LPC, p1, 1/1 RC, p6.

Row 5 K6, p2, k1, p1, k2, [wyif, drop double yo, sl 1 purlwise] 3 times, sl 3 sts back to LH needle and p3tog tbl, k4.

Row 6 P4, 1/1 LPC, p1, k1, 1/1 RPC, 1/1 LPC, p5.

Row 7 K5, p1, k2, p2, k1, p1, k5.

Row 8 P5, 1/1 LPC, 1/1 RPC, p1, 1/1 RPC, p5.

Row 9 K6, p1, k2, p2, k6.

Row 10 P6, 1/1 LC, p1, 1/1 RPC, p1, [k1, yo, k1] into next st, turn and p3, turn and [k1, yo twice] 3 times, p4.

Row 11 K4, [wyif, drop double yo, sl 1 purlwise] 3 times, sl 3 sts back to LH needle and p3tog tbl, k2, p1, k1, p2, k6.

Row 12 P5, 1/1 RPC, 1/1 LPC, k1, p1, 1/1 RPC, p4.

Rep rows 1 to 12 until desired length, end with row 1.

Next row (RS) Bind off 13 sts, cut yarn and tie off rem sts on RH needle. Sl rem sts off needle and unravel them down to first row.

With RS facing, pick up and k approx 3 sts for every 4 rows along right side of edging. K 3 rows. Cont as desired.

ribs

cable and bobble horizontal

▶ (over 20 sts)

4/4 RC Sl 4 sts to cn and hold to back, k4, k4 from cn.

4/4 LC Sl 4 sts to cn and hold to front, k4, k4 from cn.

Make bobble (MB) K into front, back and front of same st—3 sts; turn, k3, turn, p3, turn, k3; pass 2nd and 3rd sts, one at a time, over first st, turn, sl rem st to RH needle.

Row 1 (RS) P1, k19.

Row 2 and all WS rows P19, k1.

Row 3 P1, 4/4 RC, MB, k1, MB, 4/4 LC.

Row 5 P1, k9, MB, k9.

Row 6 Rep row 2.

Rep rows 3 to 6 until desired length.

2/2 vertical bobble smocked rib

▲ (multiple of 9 sts plus 6)

Make bobble (MB) K into front, back, front, back and front of same st—5 sts; [turn, k5, turn, p5] twice; pass 2nd, 3rd, 4th, and 5th sts, one at a time, over first st.

Rows 1 and 5 (RS) *K2, p2, k2, p3; rep from *, end k2, p2, k2.

Rows 2, 4 and 6 *P2, k2, p2, k3; rep from *, end p2, k2, p2.

Row 3 *K2, p2, k2, p1, MB, p1; rep from *, end k2, p2, k2.

Rep rows 1 to 6 until desired length.

Cont as desired.

Smocking Thread a long length of yarn into a tapestry needle and join two sets of knit sts above the first row of bobbles as foll: Bring needle from back to front just before the first knint st on the LH side, reinsert from front to back after the last st of the 2nd set, wind the yarn once around these same sts, finising with the needle at the back. Pull yarn gently, drawing the sts tog. Carrying the yarn across back of work, smock the next two sets of knit sts as before. Cont in this way across the row. Work the next row of smocking above the 2nd row of bobbles, but alternate the knit sts by skipping the first set, then smock the next two sets.

ribbed fox cable

▶ (over 18 sts)

4/4 Rib RC Sl 4 sts to cn and hold to back, k1, p2, k1, then k1, p2, k1 from cn.

4/4 Rib LC Sl 4 sts to cn and hold to front, k1, p2, k1, then k1, p2, k1 from cn.

Rows 1, 3, 5 and 9 (RS) P1, k1, [p2, k2] 3 times, p2, k1, p1.

Row 2 and all WS rows K1, p1, [k2, p2] 3 times, k2, p1, k1.

Row 7 P1, 4/4 Rib RC, 4/4 Rib LC, p1.

Row 10 Rep row 2.

Rep rows 1 to 10 until desired length. Bind off.

wrapped rib

▲ (multiple of 6 sts plus 3)

Wrap 3 (W3) Wyif sl next 3 sts purlwise, pass yarn to back, sl same 3 sts back to LH needle, pass yarn to front, sl sts back to RH needle.

Rows 1 and 3 (RS) *P3, k3; rep from *, end p3.

Rows 2, 4 and 6 *K3, p3; rep from *, end k3.

Row 5 *P3, W3; rep from *, end p3.

Rep rows 1 to 6 until desired length.

Cont as desired.

horizontal wrapped rib

▶ (over 20 sts)

Wrap 5 (W5) Wyif sl next 5 sts purlwise, pass yarn to back, sl same 5 sts back to LH needle, pass yarn to front, sl sts back to RH needle.

Rows 1, 3 and 5 (RS) K6, [p2, k5] twice.

Rows 2, 4 and 6 [P5, k2] twice, p6.

Row 7 K1, [W5, p2] twice, W5.

Row 8 Rep row 2.

Rep rows 1 to 8 until desired length, end with row 6.

Bind off.

ribs

bamboo rib

▶ (over 17 sts)

Rows 1, 3 and 5 (RS) K5, [p2, k4] twice.

Rows 2, 4 and 6 [P4, k2] twice, p5.

Row 7 K1, [p4, k2] twice, p4.

Row 8 [K4, p2] twice, k4, p1.

Rows 9 and 10 Rep rows 1 and 2.

Rep rows 1 to 10 until desired length, end with row 4.

Bind off.

bumps

▲ (multiple of 12 sts plus 9)

Wrap 3 (W3) [Wyif sl 3 sts purlwise, pass yarn to back, sl same 3 sts back to LH needle] 4 times, wyif sl 3 sts, pass yarn to back.

Rows 1, 3 and 7 (RS) Knit.

Row 2 (WS) Knit.

Rows 4, 6, 8 and 10 Purl.

Row 5 K3, *W3, k9; rep from*, end last rep k3.

Row 9 K9, *W3, k9; rep from* to end.

Cont as desired.

1x1 vertical bobble rib

▲ (multiple of 6 sts plus 5)

Make bobble (MB) [K into front and back of same st] twice—4 sts; pass 2nd, 3rd and 4th sts, one at a time, over first st.

Rows 1 and 3 (RS) *P1, k1; rep from *, end p1.

Row 2 [K1, p1] twice, k1, *MB, [k1, p1] twice, k1; rep from * to end.

Row 4 *K1, p1; rep from *, end k1.

Rep rows 1 to 4 until desired length.

Cont as desired.

blackberry rib

▲ (multiple of 9 sts)

Note Work M1's without twisting them (that is, k into front of strand) so that eyelets are formed.

Row 1 (WS) *P5, k4; rep from * to end.

Rows 2 and 4 *P4, M1, k2tog, k1, ssk, M1; rep from * to last 9 sts, p4, M1, k2tog, k3.

Row 3 *P5, p3tog, [k1, p1, k1] into next st; rep from * to end.

Row 5 *P5, [k1, p1, k1] into next st, p3tog; rep from * to end.

Rep rows 2 to 5 until desired length.

Cont as desired.

ribs

bulbous ribs

▲ (multiple of 3 sts plus 2)

Rows 1, 3 and 5 (RS) *P2, k1; rep from *, end p2.

Rows 2, 4 and 6 *K2, p1; rep from *, end k2.

Row 7 *P2, k into back, front and back of next st; rep from *, end p2.

Rows 8 and 10 *K2, p3; rep from *, end k2.

Row 9 *P2, k3; rep from*, end p2.

Row 11 *P2, SK2P; rep from *, end p2.

Row 12 Rep row 2.

Rep rows 1 to 12 until desired length.

Cont as desired.

old bones rib

▲ (multiple of 4 sts plus 3)

Make bobble (MB) K into front, back, front, back and front of same st—5 sts; turn, k5, turn, k5tog tbl.

Row 1 (RS) *P3, MB; rep from *, end p3.

Row 2 *K3, p1 tbl; rep from *, end k3.

Rows 3, 5 and 7 (RS) *P3, k1 tbl; rep from *, end p3.

Rows 4, 6 and 8 *K3, p1 tbl; rep from *, end k3.

Row 9 *P3, [k1, yo, k1] into next st; rep from *, end p3.

Row 10 *K3, p3tog; rep from *, end k3.

Rep rows 3 to 10 until desired length, end with row 4.

Cont as desired.

1 x 1 double bobble rib

▲ (multiple of 4 sts plus 3)

• Make bobble (MB) as for 1 x 1 Bobble Rib/Fringe.

Rows 1 and 5 (RS) *P1, k1; rep from *, end p1.

Rows 2, 4 and 6 *K1, p1; rep from *, end k1.

Row 3 *P1, k1, p1, MB; rep from *, end p1, k1, p1.

Row 7 P1, *MB, p1, k1, p1; rep from *, end MB, p1.

Row 8 Rep row 2.

Rep rows 1 and 2 until desired length.

Cont as desired.

cable and bobble drop rib

▲ **Note** Cast on using knit on cast on. (beg with a multiple of 9 sts plus 3 and end with a multiple of 8 sts plus 3)

1/2 RC Sl 2 sts to cn and hold to back, k1; k2 from cn.

Make bobble (MB) [(K1, p1) twice, k1] into same st—5 sts; turn, k5, turn, p5, turn, k2tog, k1, k2tog, turn, p3tog.

Bobble edge row (WS) Cast on 7 sts, *MB into last cast-on st on LH needle, then sl st back onto LH needle, cast on 9 sts; rep from * until desired width, end last rep cast on 5 sts.

Preparation row (RS) [K1, p1] twice, *k1, k2tog tbl, [k1, p1] 3 times; rep from *, end last rep [k1, p1] twice, k1.

Rows 1 and 3 (WS) [P1, k1] twice, *p3, [k1, p1] twice, k1; rep from *, end last rep [k1, p1] twice.

Row 2 [K1, p1] twice, *1/2 RC, [p1, k1] twice, p1; rep from *, end last rep [p1, k1] twice.

Row 4 [K1, p1] twice, *k3, [p1, k1] twice, p1; rep from *, end last rep [p1, k1] twice.

Rep rows 1 to 4 until desired length.

Cont as desired.

ribs

2-color single boxed bobble

▲ (multiple of 6 sts plus 1)

Colors Orange (A) and Beige (B)

Make bobble (MB) With B, k into front, back, front and back of same st—4 sts; turn, k4, turn, p4; pass 2nd, 3rd and 4th sts, one at a time, over first st.

Cast on with A.

Row 1 (RS) With A, purl.

Rows 2, 4 and 6 (WS) With A, purl.

Rows 3 and 7 With A, p1, *k5, p1; rep from * to end.

Row 5 *With A, p1, k2, MB with B, with A, k2; rep from *, end p1 with A.

Row 8 With A, purl.

P 1 row, k 1 row.

Cont as desired.

2-color double boxed bobble

▲ (multiple of 6 sts plus 1)

Colors Orange (A) and Rust (B)

Work rows 1 to 8 of 2-color single boxed bobble twice, then work rows 1 and 2 once more.

Cont as desired.

vertical bobble st rib

▲ (multiple of 8 sts plus 3)

Make bobble (MB) [P1, k1] twice into same st—4 sts; pass 2nd, 3rd and 4th sts, one at a time, over first st.

Rows 1 and 3 (WS) P3, *k5, p3; rep from * to end.

Row 2 K3, *p2, MB, p2, k3; rep from * to end.

Row 4 K3, *p5, k3; rep from * to end.

Rep rows 1 to 4 until desired length.

Cont as desired.

3-color shirred puff st

▲ (multiple of 8 sts plus 4)

Colors Orange (A), Rust (B) and Gold (C)

Note Sl sts purlwise with yarn at WS of work.
Cast on with A.

P 1 row, k 1 row, p 1 row.

Beg 3-Color Shirred Puff St Pat

Row 1 (RS) With B, k1, sl 2, *k6, sl 2; rep from *,
end k1.

Row 2 With B, p1, sl 2, *p6, sl 2; rep from *, end p1.

Rows 3 to 6 Rep rows 1 and 2 twice more.

Row 7 With A, knit.

Row 8 With A, purl.

Row 9 With C, k5, sl 2, *k6, sl 2; rep from *,
end k5.

Row 10 With C, p5, sl 2, *p6, sl 2; rep from *,
end p5.

Rows 11 to 14 Rep rows 9 and 10 twice more.

Rows 15 and 16 Rep rows 7 and 8.

Rep rows 1 to 6 once more.

Cont as desired.

3/2 center bobble rib I

▲ (multiple of 5 sts plus 2)

Make bobble (MB) [(K1, p1)] twice, k1] into same st—5 sts; turn, p5, turn,
k5, turn, p5, turn; pass 2nd, 3rd, 4th and 5th sts, one at a time, over first st,
sl st back to RH needle.

Rows 1 and 3 (RS) P2, *k3, p2; rep from * to end.

Rows 2, 4 and 6 K2, *p3, k2; rep from * to end.

Row 5 P2, *k1, MB, k1, p2; rep from * to end.

Rep rows 1 to 6 until desired length, end with row 2.

Cont as desired.

3/2 center bobble rib II

▲ (multiple of 5 sts plus 2)

Make bobble (MB) [K1, p1] twice into same st—4
sts; turn, p4, turn, k4; pass 2nd, 3rd and 4th sts,
one at a time, over first st.

Rows 1, 3 and 7 (RS) P2, *k3, p2; rep from * to end.

Rows 2, 4 and 6 K2, *p3, k2; rep from * to end.

Row 5 P2, *k1, MB, k1, p2; rep from * to end.

Row 8 Rep row 2.

Rep rows 1 to 8 until desired length.

Cont as desired.

ribs

double bobble rows

▲ (multiple of 10 sts)

Row 1 (RS) P4, k2, *p8, k2; rep from *, end p4.

Row 2 K4, p2, *k8, p2; rep from *, end k4.

Row 3 P4, [(k1, p1, k1, p1, k1) into next st] twice, *p8, [(k1, p1, k1, p1, k1) into next st] twice; rep from *, end p4.

Row 4 K4, p10, *k8, p10; rep from *, end k4.

Row 5 P4, k10, *p8, k10; rep from *, end p4.

Row 6 K4, [p5tog] twice, *k8, [p5tog] twice; rep from *, end k4.

Rep rows 1 to 6 until desired length.

Cont as desired.

double bobble rows with bobble drop

▲ • Work as for Double Bobble Rows until desired length.

• Make bobbles separately and sew to lower edge, centered on each double bobble.

Make bobble (MB) Cast on 1 st, leaving a 4" (10cm) tail. K into front, back, front, back and front of same st—5 sts; [turn, k5, turn p5] twice, turn, k2tog, k1, k2tog, turn, p3, turn, SK2P. Fasten off, leaving a 4" (10cm) tail. Fold bobble in half and pull both tails through to WS of finished piece, knot them tog and weave in ends.

tree tops

▲ (multiple of 15 sts plus 2)

Make bobble (MB) Cast on 1 st, leaving a 4" (10cm) tail. K into front, back, front, back and front of same st—5 sts; turn, p5, turn k5, turn, p5, turn, k2tog, k1, k2tog, turn, SP2P. Fasten off, leaving a 4" (10cm) tail. Fold bobble in half and pull both tails through to WS of finished piece, knot them tog. P 1 row on WS.

Beg Tree Tops Pat

Row 1 (RS) P2, *M1, k3, p2, p3tog, p2, k3, M1, p2; rep from * to end.

Row 2 K2, *p4, k5, p4, k2; rep from * to end.

Row 3 P2, *M1, k4, p1, p3tog, p1, k4, M1, p2; rep from * to end.

Row 4 K2, *p5, k3, p5, k2; rep from * to end.

Row 5 P2, *M1, k5, p3tog, k5, M1, p2; rep from * to end.

Row 6 K2, *p6, k1, p6, k2; rep from * to end.

Rep rows 1 to 6 until desired length.

Cont as desired.

Make bobbles and attach to points at lower edge, either singly or in clusters, as shown.

arrow cable rib/bobbles

▲ (multiple of 8 sts plus 2)

Colors Orange (A) and Yellow (B)

Note Sl sts purlwise with yarn at WS of work.

Make bobble (MB) Cast on 1 st, leaving a 4" (10cm) tail. K into front, back, front, back and front of same st—5 sts; [turn, p5, turn k5] twice, pass 2nd, 3rd, 4th, and 5th sts, one at a time, over first st. Fasten off, leaving a 4" (10cm) tail. Fold bobble in half and pull both tails through to WS of finished piece, knot them tog.

Cast on with A.

Row 1 (WS) With A, k2, *p6, k2; rep from * to end.

Row 2 With A, p2, *sl 1, k4, sl 1, p2; rep from * to end.

Rows 3 and 5 With B, k2, *sl 1, p4, sl 1, k2; rep from * to end.

Row 4 With B, rep row 2.

Row 6 With B, p2, *drop sl st off needle to front of work, k2, then with LH needle, pick up sl st and knit it (taking care that sl st is not twisted); sl next 2 sts to RH needle, drop next sl st off needle to front of work, then sl the 2 sts back to LH needle, pick up dropped st with LH needle and knit it, k2, p2; rep from * to end.

Rep rows 1 to 6 until desired length. Cont as desired. Make bobbles, alternating colors, and sew to lower edge, centered on St st/sl st panels.

slip st tile/bobble

▲ (multiple of 7 sts plus 1)

Colors Rust (A) and Gold (B)

Note Sl sts purlwise with yarn at WS of work.

Make bobble (MB) Cast on 1 st, leaving a 4" (10cm) tail. K into front, back, front and back of same st—4 sts; turn, p4, turn k4, pass 2nd, 3rd and 4th sts, one at a time, over first st. Fasten off, leaving a 4" (10cm) tail. Fold bobble in half and pull both tails through to WS of finished piece, knot them tog.

Cast on with A.

Row 1 (WS) With A, k3, p2, *k5, p2; rep from *, end k3.

Rows 2 and 4 (RS) With B, k3, sl 2, *k5, sl 2; rep from *, end k3.

Rows 3 and 5 With B, p3, sl 2, *p5, sl 2; rep from *, end p3.

Row 6 With A, *k1, sl 2, drop next sl st off needle to front of work, sl same 2 sts back to LH needle, pick up dropped st with LH needle and knit it (taking care that sl st is not twisted), k2, drop next sl st off needle to front of work, k2, pick up dropped st with LH needle and knit it; rep from *, end k1.

Rep rows 1 to 6 until desired length, end with row 1. Cont as desired.

Make bobbles with A and attach to lower edge.

ribs

2-color chain rib/fringe

▲ (begs and ends with a multiple of 6 sts plus 3)

Colors Gold (A) and Orange (B)

Note Sl sts purlwise with yarn at WS of work.

Cast on with A.

Row 1 (WS) With A, k2, *p2, k1; rep from *, end p2, k2.

Row 2 With B, k1, k into front and back of next st, *sl 1, k3, sl 1, [k1, p1, k1] into next st; rep from * to last 7 sts, sl 1, k3, sl 1, k into front and back of next st, k1.

Row 3 With B, p3, *sl 1, p3; rep from * to end.

Row 4 With A, k3, *ssk, k1, k2tog, k3; rep from * to end.

Rep rows 1 to 4 until desired length. Cont as desired.

Make fringe with A and attach to lower edge.

knotted st picot

▲ (multiple of 4 sts plus 2)

Cross 2 L K2, [yo, pass 2nd st on RH needle over the first st and the yo] twice

Rows 1, 3, 7, 9 and 11 (RS) Knit.

Row 2 and all WS rows Purl.

Row 5 (picot row) K1, *k2tog, yo; rep from *, end k1.

Row 13 *K2, Cross 2 L; rep from *, end k2.

Rows 14 and 16 Purl.

Row 15 Knit.

Rep rows 13 to 16 until desired length.

Cont as desired.

Fold hem to WS at picot row and sew in place.

slip st tweed

▲ (multiple of 14 sts plus 9)

Note Sl sts purlwise with yarn at WS of work.

Colors Orange (A) and Rust (B)

Cast on with A. K 2 rows.

Row 1 (RS) With B, k1, *sl 1, k5, [sl 1, k3] twice; rep from * to last 8 sts, sl 1, k5, sl 1, k1.

Row 2 With B, k1, *sl 1, k5, [sl 1, p3] twice; rep from * to last 8 sts, sl 1, k5, sl 1, k1.

Row 3 With A, k1, *[k3, sl 1] twice, k5, sl 1; rep from * to last 8 sts, k3, sl 1, k4.

Row 4 With A, k1, *[p3, sl 1] twice, k5, sl 1; rep from * to last 8 sts, p3, sl 1, p3, k1.

Rep rows 1 to 4 until desired length.

Cont as desired.

slip st tweed

▲ (multiple of 4 sts plus 3)

Note Sl sts purlwise with yarn at WS of work.

Colors Rust (A) and Orange (B)

Cast on with A.

K 1 row on WS.

Rows 1 and 2 With B, k3, *sl 1, k3; rep from * to end.

Rows 3 and 4 With A, k1, *sl 1, k3; rep from *, end sl 1, k1.

Rep rows 1 to 4 until desired length.

Cont as desired.

ribs

slip st ladder

▲ (multiple of 6 sts plus 5)

Note Sl sts purlwise with yarn at WS of work.

Colors Rust (A) and Orange (B)

Cast on with A.

P 1 row on WS.

Row 1 (RS) With B, [k1, sl 1] twice, *k3, sl 1, k1, sl 1; rep from *, end k1.

Row 2 With B, [k1, sl 1] twice, *p3, sl 1, k1, sl 1; rep from *, end k1.

Row 3 With A, k1, *k3, sl 1, k1, sl 1; rep from *, end k4.

Row 4 With A, k1, *p3, sl 1, k1, sl 1; rep from *, end p3, k1.

Rep rows 1 to 4 until desired length.

Cont as desired.

raspberries

▲ (multiple of 4 sts plus 1)

Colors Light Orange (A) and Dark Orange (B)

Note Sl sts purlwise with yarn at WS of work.

Cast on with A. Work 4 rows in St st.

Row 1 (RS) With B, knit.

Row 2 With B, purl.

Row 3 With A, k1, *sl 3, [k1, yo, k1] into next st; rep from *, end sl 3, k1.

Row 4 With A, k1, *sl 3, k3; rep from *, end sl 3, k1.

Row 5 With B, k1, *SK2P, sl 3; rep from *, end SK2P, k1.

Row 6 With B, k1, *[p1, yo, p1] into next st, sl 3; rep from *, end [p1, yo, p1] into next st, k1.

Row 7 With A, k1, *sl 3, p3; rep from *, end sl 3, k1.

Row 8 With A, k1, *sl 3, p3tog; rep from *, end sl 3, k1.

Rows 9 and 10 Rep rows 1 and 2.

Row 11 With A, k3, *sl 3, [k1, yo, k1] into next st; rep from *, end sl 3, k3.

Row 12 With A, k3, *sl 3, k3; rep from * to end.

Row 13 With B, k3, *SK2P, sl 3; rep from *, end SK2P, k3.

Row 14 With B, p3, *[p1, yo, p1] into next st, sl 3; rep from *, end [p1, yo, p1] into next st, p3.

Row 15 With A, k3, *sl 3, p3; rep from *, end sl 3, k3.

Row 16 With A, k3, *sl 3, p3tog; rep from *, end sl 3, k3.

Rep rows 1 to 16 until desired length.

Cont as desired.

Fold first 4 St st rows to WS and sew in place.

puff st

▲ (multiple of 4 sts)

Rows 1 and 3 (RS) Purl.

Row 2 *[K1, p1, k1] into next st, p3tog; rep from * to end.

Row 4 *P3tog, [k1, p1, k1] into next st; rep from * to end.

Rep rows 1 to 4 until desired length.

Cont as desired.

puff st/rolled edge

▲ (multiple of 4 sts plus 2)

Work 6 rows in St st.

Work puff st as above.

Cont as desired.

ribs

3-color fluted st

▲ **Colors** Gold (A), Orange (B) and Yellow (C)

Notes 1 Work 2 rows with each color, alternating A, B and C.

2 Sl sts purlwise with yarn at WS of work.

(multiple of 4 sts plus 1)

Cast on with A.

Row 1 (WS) P1, *k1, sl 1, k1, p1; rep from * to end.

Row 2 K1, *sl 1, p1, sl 1, k1; rep from * to end.

Rep rows 1 and 2, changing colors every 2 rows, until desired length.

Cont as desired.

3-color puff st

▲ (multiple of 4 sts plus 2)

Colors Gold (A), Orange (B) and Rust (C)

Cast on with A.

Work 4 rows in St st.

With B, work 2 rows in St st.

Work as for Puff St in the foll color sequence: With B, work rows 1 and 2.

With C, work rows 3 and 4. With A, work rows 1 and 2. With B, work rows 3 and 4. With C, work rows 1 and 2. With A, work rows 3 and 4.

Cont as desired.

accolades

▲ (multiple of 3 sts plus 2)

1/2 RC Sl 2 sts to cn and hold to back, k1, k2 from cn.

1/2 LC Sl 1 st to cn and hold to front, k2, k1 from cn.

Work 4 rows in St st.

Row 1 (RS) K1, *1/2 LC; rep from *, end k1.

Rows 2 and 4 Purl.

Row 3 K1, *1/2 RC; rep from *, end k1.

Row 5 Knit.

Row 6 Purl.

Rep rows 1 to 6 until desired length, end with row 4.

Cont as desired.

Fold first 4 rows to WS and sew in place.

waverly

▲ (multiple of 3 sts)

Note Sl sts purlwise with yarn at WS of work.

1/2 RC Sl 2 sts to cn, hold to back, k1, k2 from cn.

1/2 LC Sl 1 st to cn, hold to front, k2, k1 from cn.

P 1 row, k 1 row, p 1 row.

Beg Waverly Pat

Row 1 (RS) K2, *sl 1, k2; rep from * to last st, k1.

Row 2 P3, *sl 1, p2; rep from * to end.

Row 3 K2, *1/2 LC; rep from *, end k1.

Rows 4 and 6 Purl.

Row 5 K2, *yo, k2tog, k1; rep from * to last st, k1.

Row 7 K4, *sl 1, k2; rep from *, end sl 1, k1.

Row 8 P1, *sl 1, p2; rep from * to last 2 sts, p2.

Row 9 K2, *1/2 RC; rep from *, end k1.

Row 10 Knit.

Rows 11 and 12 Purl.

Rep rows 1 to 12 until desired length.

Cont as desired.

twisted openwork

▲ (multiple of 4 sts plus 1)

Rows 1 and 3 (RS) P1, *k3, p1; rep from * to end.

Row 2 *K1, p3; rep from *, end k1.

Row 4 K1, *yo, p3tog, yo, k1; rep from * to end.

Rows 5 and 7 K2, p1, *k3, p1; rep from *, end k2.

Row 6 P2, k1, *p3, k1; rep from *, end p2.

Row 8 P2tog, yo, k1, *yo, p3tog, yo, k1; rep from * to last
2 sts, yo, p2tog.

Rep rows 1 to 8 until desired length.

Cont as desired.

vertical bobble st rib

▲ (multiple of 8 sts plus 3)

Make bobble (MB) [P1, k1] twice into same st—4 sts; pass 2nd,
3rd and 4th sts, one at a time, over first st.

Rows 1 and 3 (WS) P3, *k5, p3; rep from * to end.

Row 2 K3, *p2, MB, p2, k3; rep from * to end.

Row 4 K3, *p5, k3; rep from * to end.

Rep rows 1 to 4 until desired length.

Cont as desired.

vertical openwork

 (multiple of 4 sts)

Row 1 (RS) *K2, yo, ssk; rep from * to end.

Row 2 *P2, yo, p2tog; rep from * to end.

Rep rows 1 and 2 until desired length.

Cont as desired.

openwork rib

 (multiple of 6 sts plus 3)

Row 1 (RS) *P3, yo, SK2P, yo; rep from *, end p3.

Row 2 K3, *p3, k3; rep from * to end.

Rep rows 1 and 2 until desired length.

Cont as desired.

ribs

lattice rib

(multiple of 6 sts plus 3)

K3W K3 wrapping yarn twice around needle for each st.

Work 5 rows in St st.

Beg Lattice Rib Pat

Row 1 (WS) P3, *K3W, p3; rep from * to end.

Row 2 K3, *p3 (dropping extra loops), k3; rep from * to end.

Rep rows 1 and 2 until desired length.

Cont as desired.

lattice rib reversed

garter drop st

▲ (any number of sts)

Work 5 rows in St st. K 1 row on WS for turning ridge.

K 2 rows.

Beg Garter Drop St Pat

Row 1 (RS) *K1 wrapping yarn 3 times around needle; rep from *
to end.

Row 2 Knit, dropping extra loops.

Rows 3 to 6 Knit.

Rep rows 1 to 6 until desired length, end with row 2.

Cont as desired.

Fold hem to WS at turning ridge and sew in place.

spot rib

▲ (multiple of 4 sts plus 1)

Rows 1 and 3 (RS) *K1, p3; rep from *, end k1.

Rows 2 and 4 P1, *k3, p1; rep from * to end.

Row 5 *K1, p2tog, yo, p1; rep from *, end k1.

Row 6 Rep row 2.

Rep rows 1 to 6 until desired length.

Cont as desired.

eyelet rib

(multiple of 8 sts plus 2) ◪

• Use either knit or purl side as the RS of work.

Row 1 *P2, k2; rep from *, end p2.

Row 2 K2, p2, *yo, k2tog, p2; rep from *, end k2.

Rep rows 1 and 2 four times more.

Row 3 P2, *k6, p2; rep from * to end.

Row 4 K2, p6, *yo, k2tog, p6; rep from *, end k2.

Rep rows 3 and 4 until desired length.

Cont as desired.

ribs

caterpillar eyelet rib

▲ (multiple of 6 sts plus 2)

Row 1 (RS) *P2, k2tog, yo, k2; rep from *, end p2.

Row 2 K2, *p2tog, yo, p2, k2; rep from * to end.

Rep rows 1 and 2 until desired length.

Cont as desired.

wide vertical eyelet

▲ (multiple of 10 sts plus 2)

Row 1 (RS) K2, *yo, k2tog, k4, ssk, yo, k2; rep from * to end.

Row 2 Purl.

Rep rows 1 and 2 until desired length.

Cont as desired.

mock cable

▲ (multiple of 3 sts plus 2)

Row 1 (RS) *P2, M1, k1, M1; rep from *, end p2.

Row 2 K2, *p3, k2; rep from * to end.

Row 3 *P2, k3; rep from *, end p2.

Row 4 K2, *p3tog, k2; rep from * to end.

Rep rows 1 to 4 until desired length.

Cont as desired.

mock cable eyelet

▲ (multiple of 9 sts plus 2)

Note Work M1s without twisting them (that is, k through front of strand) so that eyelets are formed.

Row 1 (RS) *P2, ssk, M1, k3, M1, k2tog; rep from *, end p2.

Rows 2 and 4 K2, *p7, k2; rep from * to end.

Row 3 *P2, k2, M1, SK2P, M1, k2; rep from *, end p2.

Rep rows 1 to 4 until desired length.

Cont as desired.

ribs

slip st rib

▲ (multiple of 3 sts)

Row 1 (WS) *P2, wyib insert RH needle from front to back under strand between last st worked and next st on LH needle, wrap yarn knitwise around RH needle and pull up a loop, k1; rep from * to end.

Row 2 *P1, wyif sl 1 purlwise, k2, psso the k2 sts; rep from * to end.

Rep rows 1 and 2 until desired length.

Cont as desired.

wrap eyelet rib

▲ (multiple of 3 sts)

Row 1 (RS) *Wyif sl 1 purlwise, k2, psso the k2; rep from * to end.

Row 2 Purl.

Rep rows 1 and 2 until desired length.

Cont as desired.

shell eyelet rib

▲ (multiple of 6 sts plus 5)

Row 1 (RS) P1, *p3, yo, k3tog, yo; rep from *, end p4.

Row 2 K4, *p3, k3; rep from *, end k1.

Row 3 P1, *yo, k3tog, yo, p3; rep from *, end last rep p1.

Row 4 K1, p3, *k3, p3; rep from *, end k1.

Rep rows 1 to 4 until desired length.

Cont as desired.

duck foot rib

▲ (multiple of 5 sts plus 3)

Rows 1 and 5 (RS) *P3, k2; rep from *, end p3.

Rows 2, 4 and 6 *K3, p2; rep from *, end k3.

Row 3 *P3, k2tog, yo; rep from *, end p3.

Row 7 *P3, yo, ssk; rep from *, end p3.

Row 8 Rep row 2.

Rep rows 1 to 8 until desired length.

Cont as desired.

ribs

bridge eyelet mock rib

▲ (multiple of 5 sts plus 3)

Rows 1 and 3 (RS) *K3, yo, k2tog; rep from *, end k3.

Row 2 P3, *k1, p4; rep from * to end.

Row 4 Purl.

Rep rows 1 to 4 until desired length.

Cont as desired.

ribbon eyelet rib

▲ (multiple of 6 sts plus 4)

Row 1 (RS) *K4, yo, k2tog; rep from *, end k4.

Row 2 *P4, yo, p2tog; rep from *, end p4.

Rep rows 1 and 2 until desired length.

Cont as desired.

Run a matching ribbon up through one vertical line of eyelets, then down through 2nd vertical row. Knot ribbon ends at WS of work. Rep for all pairs of vertical eyelet lines.

tree of life welt

 (multiple of 13 sts plus 4)

1/1 RPC Sl 1 st to cn and hold to back, k1 tbl, p1 from cn.

1/1 LPC Sl 1 st to cn and hold to front, p1, k1 tbl from cn.

K 1 row on WS.

Row 1 *K4, p3, k3 tbl, p 3; rep from * to last 4 sts, k4.

Row 2 P4, *k3, p3 tbl, k3, p4; rep from * to end.

Row 3 *K4, p2, 1/1RPC, k 1 tbl, 1/1LPC, p2; rep from * to last 4 sts, k4.

Row 4 P4, *k2, [p1 tbl, k1] twice, p1 tbl, k2, p4; rep from * to end.

Row 5 *K4, p1, 1/1RPC, p1, k1b, p1, 1/1LPC, p1; rep form * to last 4 sts, k4.

Row 6 P4, * k1, p1 tbl, [k2, p1 tbl] twice, k1, p4; rep from * to end.

Row 7 *K4, 1/1RPC, p1, k3 tbl, p1, 1/1LPC; rep from * to last 4 sts, k4.

Row 8 P4, * p1 tbl, k2, p3 tbl, k 2, p1 tbl, p4; rep from * to end.

Row 9 *K4, p2, 1/1RPC, k1b, 1/1LPC, p2; rep from * to last 4 sts, k4.

Rows 10 to 13 Rep rows 4 to 7.

Row 14 (WS) Knit.

Cont as desired.

zig zag welt

 (multiple of 7 sts plus 4)

K 1 row on WS.

Row 1 *K4, k1 tbl, p2; rep from * to last 4 sts, k4.

Row 2 P4, *k2, p1 tbl, p4; rep from * to end.

Row 3 *K4, 1/1LPC (see above), p1; rep from * to last 4 sts, k4.

Row 4 P4, * k1, p1 tbl, k1, p4; rep from * to end.

Row 5 *K4, p1, 1/1LPC; rep from * to last 4 sts, k4.

Row 6 P4, *p1 tbl, k2, p4; rep from * to end.

Row 7 *K4, p1, 1/1RPC (see above); rep from * to last 4 sts, k4.

Row 8 P4, * k1, p1 tbl, k1, p4; rep from * to end.

Row 9 *K4, 1/1RPC, p1; rep from * to last 4 sts, k4.

Rows 10 to 17 Rep rows 2 to 9.

Rows 18 and 19 Knit.

Cont as desired.

slanting welt

▲ (multiple of 6 sts plus 3)

1/1 LPC Sl 1 st to cn and hold to front, p1, k1 tbl from cn.

K 1 row on WS.

Row 1 *K3, k1 tbl, p2; rep from * to last 3 sts, k3.

Row 2 P3, * k2, p1 tbl, p3; rep from * to end.

Row 3 *K3, 1/1LPC, p1; rep from * to last 3 sts, k3.

Row 4 P3, * k1, p1 tbl, k 1, p3; rep from * to end.

Row 5 *K3, p1, 1/1LPC; rep from * to last 3 sts, k3.

Row 6 P3, *p1 tbl, k2, p3; rep from * to end.

Rep rows 1 to 6 twice more.

K 2 rows. Cont as desired.

cassie's combo

▲ (multiple of 24 sts)

2/2 RC Sl 2 sts to cn and hold to back, k2, k2 from cn.

2/2 LC Sl 2 sts to cn and hold to front, k2, k2 from cn.

Foundation row (WS) *K2, p4, k2, p8, k2, p4, k2; rep from * to end.

Rows 1 (RS) *P2, k4, p12, k4, p2; rep from * to end.

Row 2 *K2, p4, k12, p4, k2; rep from * to end.

Row 3 *P2, k4, p2, k8, p2, k4, p2; rep from * to end.

Row 4 *K2, p4, k2, p8, k2, p4, k2; rep from * to end.

Row 5 *P2, 2/2RC, p2, 2/2RC, 2/2LC, p2, 2/2LC, p2; rep from * to end.

Row 6 *K2, p4, k2, p8, k2, p4; rep from * to end.

Row 7 *P2, k4, p2, k8, p2, k4, p2; rep from * to end.

Row 8 *K2, p4, k2, p8, k2, p4, k2; rep from * to end.

Row 9 *P2, 2/2RC, p2, 2/2LC, 2/2RC, p2, 2/2LC, p2; rep from * to end.

Row 10 *K2, p4, k2, p8, k2, p4, k2; rep from * to end.

Row 11 *P2, k4, p12, k 4, p2; rep from * to end.

Row 12 K2, p4, k12, p4, k2; rep from * to end.

Row 13 Purl.

Cont as desired.

bell & lace

▲ (multiple of 12 sts plus 5)

K 1 row on WS.

Row 1 (RS) P2, * k1, p4, k3, p4; rep from * end k1, p2.

Row 2 K2, p1, * k4, p3, k4, p1; rep from * end k2.

Row 3 P2 * [(k1,p1)twice, k1] all in next st, p4, yo, Sk2P, yo, p4; rep from * end [(k1,p1) twice, k1] all in next st, p2.

Row 4 K2, p5, * k4, p3, k4, p5; rep from * end k2.

Row 5 P2, * k5, p4, k3, p4; rep from *, end k5, p2.

Row 6 K2, p5, * k4, p3, k4, p5; rep from *, end k2.

Row 7 P2, * k5, p4, yo, Sk2P, yo, p4; rep from *, end k5, p2.

Row 8 K2, p5, * k4, p3, k4, p5; rep from * end k2.

Row 9 P2, * k 5 tog, p4, k3, p4; rep from * end k5 tog, p2.

Row 10 K2, p1, * k4, p3, k4, p1; rep from * end k2.

Row 11 P2, * k1, p4, yo, Sk2P, yo, p4; rep from *, end k1, p2.

Row 12 K2, p1, * k4, p3, k4, p1; rep from * end k2.

Rows 13 to 24 Rep rows 1 to 12.

Row 25 Purl.

Cont as desired.

garter stitch and cable pattern

▲ (multiple of 20 sts plus 14)

3/3 RC

K 1 row on WS.

Row 1 (RS) *P1, k2, p1, k6, p1, k2, p1, k6; rep from * to last 14 sts, end p1, k2, p1, k6, p1, k2, p1.

Row 2 K4, p6, k4, * p6, k4, p6, k4; rep from * across to end.

Row 3 Rep row 1.

Row 4 Rep row 2.

Row 5 * P1, k2, p1, 3/3 RC, p1, k2, p1, k6; rep from * to last 14 sts, end p1, k2, p1, 3/3 RC, p1, k2, p1.

Row 6 Rep row 2.

Row 7 Rep row 1.

Row 8 Rep row 2.

Rows 9 to 16 Rep rows 1 to 8.

Row 17 Rep row 1.

Row 18 (WS) Knit.

Cont as desired.

bobble diamond and cables

▲ (multiple of 19 sts plus 6)

RT K 2nd st passing in front of first, then k first st.

5 in 1 ([K1, p1] twice, k1) all in next st.

Row 1 (WS) K2, p2, k2, *p6, 5 in 1, p6, k2, p2, k2; rep from * to end.

Row 2 *P2, RT, p2, k6, k5tog, k6; rep from * end p2, RT, p2.

Row 3 K2, p2, k2, * p5, 5 in 1, p1, 5 in 1, p5, k2, p2, k2; rep from * to end.

Row 4 *P2, k2, p2, k5, k5tog, k1, k5tog, k5; rep form *, end p2, k2, p2.

Row 5 K2, p2, k2, *p4, [5 in 1, p1] twice, 5 in 1, p4, k2, p2, k2; rep from * to end.

Row 6 *P2, RT, p2, k4, [k5tog, k1] twice, k5tog, k4; rep from * end p2, RT p2.

Row 7 K2, p2, k2, *p3, [5 in 1, p1] 3 times, 5 in 1, p3, k2, p2, k2; rep from * to end.

Row 8 *P2, k2, p2, k3, [k5tog, k1] 3 times, k5tog, k3; rep from *, end p2, k2, p2.

Row 9 K2, p2, k2, *p2, [5 in 1, p1] 4 times, 5 in 1, p2, k2, p2, k2; rep from * to end.

Row 10 *P2, RT, p2, k2, [k5tog, k1] 4 times, k5tog, k2; rep from *, end p2, RT, p2.

Row 11 K2, p2, k2, *p1, [5 in 1, p1] 5 times, 5 in 1, p1, k2, p2, k2; rep from * to end.

Row 12 *P2, k2, p2, k1, [k5tog, k1] 5 times, k5tog, k1; rep from *, end p2, k2, p2.

Row 13 Rep row 9.

Row 14 Rep row 10.

Row 15 Rep row 7.

Rows 16 Rep row 8.

Row 17 Rep row 5.

Row18 Rep row 6.

Row 19 Rep row 3.

Row 20 Rep row 4.

Row 21 Rep row 1.

Row 22 Rep row 2.

Row 23 (WS) Knit.

Cont as desired.

honeycomb and bell wave

▲ (multiple of 16 sts plus 8)

1/1 RC Sl 1 st to cn and hold to back, k1, k1 from cn.

1/1 LC Sl 1 st to cn and hold to front, k1, k1 from cn.

2/1 RPC Sl 1 st to cn and hold to back, k2, p1 from cn.

2/1 LPC Sl 2 sts to cn and hold to front, p1, k2 from cn.

Row 1 (WS) K2, p4, *k2, p2, k8, p4; rep from * to last 2 sts, k2.

Row 2 P2, *1/1 LC, 1/1 RC, p7, 2/1 RPC, p2; rep from * to last 6 sts, 1/1 LC, 1/1 RC, p2.

Row 3 K2, p4, *k3, p2, k7, p4; rep from * to last 2 sts, k2.

Row 4 P2, *1/1 RC, 1/1 LC, p6, 2/1 RPC, p3; rep from * to last 6 sts, 1/1 RC, 1/1 LC, p2.

Row 5 K2, p4, *k4, p2, k6, p4; rep from * to last 2 sts, k2.

Row 6 P2, *1/1 LC, 1/1 RC, p5, 2/1 RPC, p4; rep from * to last 6 sts, 1/1 LC, 1/1 RC, p2.

Row 7 K2, p4, *k5, p2, k5, p4; rep from * to last 2 sts, k2.

Row 8 P2, *1/1 RC, 1/1 LC, p4, 2/1 RPC, p5; rep from * to last 6 sts, 1/1 RC, 1/1 LC, p2.

Row 9 K2, p4, *k6, p2, k4, p4; rep from * to last 2 sts, k2.

Row 10 P2, *1/1 LC, 1/1 RC, p3, 2/1 RPC, p6; rep from * to last 6 sts, 1/1 LC, 1/1 RC, p2.

Row 11 K2, p4, *k7, p2, k3, p4; rep from * to last 2 sts, k2.

Row 12 P2, *1/1 RC, 1/1 LC, p2, 2/1 RPC, p1, ([k1, p1] twice, k1) in next st, p5; rep from * to last 6 sts, 1/1 RC, 1/1 LC, p2.

Row 13 K2, p4, *k5, p5, k2, p2, k2, p4; rep from * to last 2 sts, k2.

Row 14 P2, *1/1 LC, 1/1 RC, p2, k2, p2, k5, p5; rep from * to last 6 sts, 1/1 LC, 1/1 RC, p2.

Row 15 K2, p4, *k5, p5, k2, p2, k2, p4; rep from * to last 2 sts, k2.

Row 16 P2, *1/1 RC, 1/1 LC, p2, 2/1 LPC, p1, k5tog, p5; rep from * to last 6 sts 1/1 RC, 1/1 LC, p2.

Row 17 K2, p4, *k7, p2, k3, p4; rep from * to last 2 sts, k2.

Row 18 P2, *1/1 LC, 1/1 RC, p3, 2/1 LPC, p6; rep from * to last 6 sts, 1/1 LC, 1/1 RC, p2.

Row 19 K2, p4, *k6, p2, k4, p4; rep from * to last 2 sts, k2.

Row 20 P2, *1/1 RC, 1/1 LC, p4, 2/1 LPC, p5; rep from * to last 6 sts, 1/1 RC, 1/1 LC, p2.

Row 21 K2, p4, *k5, p2, k5, p4; rep from * to last 2 sts, k2.

Row 22 P2, *1/1 LC, 1/1 RC, p5, 2/1 LPC, p4; rep from * to last 6 sts, 1/1 LC, 1/1 RC, p2.

Row 23 K2, p4, *k4, p2, k6, p4; rep from * to last 2 sts, k2.

Row 24 P2, *1/1 RC, 1/1 LC, p6, 2/1 LPC, p3; rep from * to last 6 sts, 1/1 RC, 1/1 LC, p2.

Row 25 K2, p4, *k3, p2, k7, p4; rep from * to last 2 sts, k2.

Row 26 P2, *1/1 LC, 1/1 RC, p5, ([k1, p1] twice, k1) in next st, p1, 2/1 LPC, p2; rep from * to last 6 sts, 1/1 LC, 1/1 RC, p2.

Row 27 K2, p4, *k2, p2, k2, p5, k5, p4; rep from * to last 2 sts, k2.

Row 28 P2, *1/1 RC, 1/1 LC, p5, k5, p2, k2, p2; rep from * to last 6 sts, 1/1 RC, 1/1 LC, p2.

Row 29 K2, p4, *k2, p2, k2, p5, k5, p4; rep from * to last 2 sts, k2.

Row 30 P2, *1/1 LC, 1/1 RC, p5, k5tog, p1, 2/1 RPC, p2; rep from * to last 6 sts, 1/1 LC, 1/1 RC, p2.

Row 31 K2, p4, *k3, p2, k7, p4; rep from * to last 2 sts, k2.

Row 32 P2, *1/1 RC, 1/1 LC, p6, 2/1 RPC, p3; rep from * to last 6 sts, 1/1 RC, 1/1 LC, p2.

Row 33 K2, p4, *k4, p2, k6, p4; rep from * to last 2 sts, k2.

Row 34 P2, *1/1 LC, 1/1 RC, p5, 2/1 RPC, p4; rep from * to last 6 sts, 1/1 LC, 1/1 RC, p2.

Row 35 K2, p4, *k5, p2, k5, p4; rep from * to last 2 sts, k2.

Cont as desired.

diamond and cable

▲ (multiple of 27 sts plus 30)

2/1 RPC Sl 1 st to cn and hold to back, k2, p1 from cn.

2/1 LPC Sl 2 sts to cn and hold to front, p1, k2 from cn.

3/3 LC Sl 3 sts to cn and hold to front, k3, k3 from cn.

Foundation row (WS) Sl 1, p3, [k1, p1] 4 times, *p6, [p1, k1] 4 times, p5, [k1, p1] 4 times; rep from * to last 18 sts, p6, [p1, k1] 4 times, p4.

Row 1 Sl 1, k1 tbl, 2/1 LPC, k1, [p1, k1] 3 times, k6, *[k1, p1] 3 times, k1, 2/1 RPC, k1 tbl, 2/1 LPC, k1, [p1, k1] 3 times, k6; rep from * to last 12 sts, [kl, p1] 3 times, k1, 2/1 RPC, k1 tbl, k1.

Row 2 Sl 1, p1, k1, p2, [k1, p1] 3 times, k1, *p6, [k1, p1] 3 times, k1, p2, k1, p1, k1, p2, [k1, p1] 3 times, k1; rep from * to last 18 sts, p6, [k1, p1] 3 times, k1, p2, k1, p2.

Row 3 Sl 1, k1 tbl, p1, 2/1 LPC, [k1, p1] 3 times, k6, *[p1, k1] 3 times, 2/1 RPC, p1, k1 tbl, p1, 2/1 LPC, [k1, p1] 3 times, k6; rep from * to last 12 sts, [p1, k1] 3 times, 2/1 RPC, p1, k1 tbl, k1.

Row 4 Sl 1, p1, k2, p2, [k1, p1] 3 times, *p6, [p1, k1] 3 times, p2, k2, p1, k2, p2, [k1, p1] 3 times; rep from * to last 18 sts, p6, [p1, k1] 3 times, p2, k2, p2.

Row 5 Sl 1, k1 tbl, p2, 2/1 LPC, [kl, p1] 2 times, k7, *[k1, p1] 2 times, k1, 2/1 RPC, p2, k1 tbl, p2, 2/1 LPC, [k1, p1] 2 times, k7; rep from * to last 12 sts, [k1, p1] 2 times, k1, 2/1 RPC, p2, k1 tbl, k1.

Row 6 Sl 1, p1, k3, p2, [k1, p1] 2 times, k1, *p6, [k1, p1] 2 times, k1, p2, k3, p1, k3, p2, [k1, p1] 2 times, k1; rep from * to last 18 sts, p6, [k1, p1] 2 times, k1, p2, k3, p2.

Row 7 Sl 1, k1 tbl, p3, 2/1 LPC, [k1, p1] 2 times, 3/3 LC, *[p1, k1] 2 times, 2/1 RPC, p3, k1 tbl, p3, 2/1 LPC, [k1, p1] 2 times, 3/3 LC; rep from * to last 12 sts, [p1, k1] 2 times, 2/1 RPC, p3, k1 tbl, k1.

Row 8 Sl 1, p1, k4, p2, [k1, p1] 2 times, *p6, [p1, k1] 2 times, p2, k4, p1, k4, p2, [k1, p1] 2 times; rep from * to last 18 sts, p6, [p1, k1] 2 times, p2, k4, p2.

Row 9 Sl 1, k1 tbl, p4, 2/1 LPC, k1, p1, k1, k6, *k1, p1, k1, 2/1 RPC, p4, k1 tbl, p4, 2/1 LPC, k1, p1, k1, k6; rep from * to last 12 sts, k1, p1, k1, 2/1 RPC, p4, k1 tbl, k1.

Row 10 Sl 1, p1, k5, p2, k1, p1, k1, *p6, k1, p1, k1, p2, k5, p1, k5, p2, k1, p1, k1; rep from * to last 18 sts, p6, k1, p1, k1, p2, k5, p2.

Row 11 Sl 1, k1 tbl, p2, (k1, p1, k1) all in next st, p2, 2/1 LPC, k1, p1, k6, *p1, k1, 2/1 RPC, p2, (k1, p1, k1) all in next st, p2, k1 tbl, p2, (k1, p1, k1) all in next st, p2, 2/1 LPC, k1, p1, k6; rep from * to last 12 sts, p1, k1, 2/1 RPC, p2, (k1, p1, k1) all in next st, p2, k1 tbl, k1.

Row 12 Sl 1, p1, k2, p3, k3, p2, k1, p1, *p6, p1, k1, p2, k3, p3, k2, p1, k2, p3, k3, p2, k1, p1; rep from * to last 20 sts, p6, p1, k1, p2, k3, p3, k2, p2.

Row 13 Sl 1, k1 tbl, p2, k3, p3, *2/1 LPC, k7, * k1, 2/1 RPC, p3, k3, p2, k1 tbl, p2, k3, p3, 2/1 LPC, k7; rep from * to last 14 sts, k1, 2/1 RPC, p3, k3, p2, k1 tbl, k1.

Row 14 Sl 1, p1, k2, p3, k4, p2, k1, *p6, k1, p2, k4, p3, k2, p1, k2, p3, k4, p2, k1; rep from * to last 20 sts, p6, k1, p2, k4, p3, k2, p2.

Row 15 Sl 1, k1 tbl, p 2, SK2P, p3, 2/1 RPC, p1, 3/3 LC, *p1, 2/1 LPC, p3, SK2P, p2, k1 tbl, p2, SK2P, p3, 2/1 RPC, p1, 3/3 LC; rep from * to last 14 sts, p1, 2/1 LPC, p3, SK2P, p2, k1 tbl, k1.

Row 16 Sl 1, p1, k6, p2, k1, p1, *p7, k1, p2, k6, p1, k6, p2, k1, p1; rep from * to last 18 sts, p7, k1, p2, k6, p2.

Row 17 Sl 1, k1 tbl, p5, 2/1 RPC, p1, k7, *k1, p1, 2/1 LPC, p5, k1 tbl, p5, 2/1 RPC, p1, k7; rep from * to last 12 sts, k1, p1, 2/1 LPC, p5, k1 tbl, k1.

ribs

Row 18 SI 1, p1, k5, p2, k1, p1, k1, *p6, k1, p1, k1, p2, k5, p1, k5, p2, k1, p1, k1; rep from * to last 18 sts, p6, k1, p1, k1, p2, k5, p2.

Row 19 SI 1, k1 tbl, p4, 2/1 RPC, p1, k1, p1, k6, *p1, k1, p1, 2/1 LPC, p4, k1 tbl, p4, 2/1 RPC, p1, k1, p1, k6; rep from * to last 12 sts, p1, k1, p1, 2/1 LPC, p4, k1 tbl, k1.

Row 20 SI 1, p1, k4, p2, [k1, p1] twice, *p6, [p1, k1] twice, p2, k4, p1, k4, p2 [k1, p1] twice; rep from * to last 18 sts, p6, [p1, k1] twice, p2, k4, p2.

Row 21 SI 1, k1 tbl, p3, 2/1 RPC, [p1, k1] twice, k6, *[k1, p1] twice, 2/1 LPC, p3, k1 tbl, p3, 2/1 RPC, [p1, k1] twice, k6; rep from * to last 12 sts, [k1, p1] twice, 2/1 LPC, p3, k1 tbl, k1.

Row 22 SI 1, p1, k3, p2, [k1, p1] twice, k1, *p6, [k1, p1] twice, k1, p2, k3, p1, k3, p2, [k1, p1] twice, k1; rep from * to last 18 sts, p6, [k1, p1] twice, k1, p2, k3, p2.

Row 23 SI 1, k1 tbl, p2, 2/1 RPC, [p1, k1] twice, p1, 3/3 LC, *[p1, k1] twice, p1, 2/1 LPC, p2, k1 tbl, p2, 2/1 RPC, [p1, k1] twice, p1, 3/3 LC; rep from * to last 12 sts, [p1, k1] twice, p1, 2/1 LPC, p2, k1 tbl, k1.

Row 24 SI 1, p1, k2, p2, [k1, p1] 3 times, *p6, [p1, k1] 3 times, p2, k2, p1, k2, p2, [k1, p1] 3 times; rep from * to last 18 sts, p6, [p1, k1] 3 times, p2, k2, p2.

Row 25 SI 1, k1 tbl, p1, 2/1 RPC, [p1, k1] 3 times, k6, *[k1, p1] 3 times, 2/1 LPC, p1, k1 tbl, p1, 2/1 RPC, [p1, k1] 3 times, k6; rep from * to last 12 sts, [k1, p1] 3 times, 2/1 LPC, p1, k1 tbl, k1.

Row 26 SI 1, p1, k1, p2, [k1, p1] 3 times, k1, *p6, [k1, p1] 3 times, k1, p2, k1, p1, k1, p2, [k1, p1] 3 times, k1; rep from * to last 18 sts, p6, [k1, p1] 3 times, k1, p2, k1, p2.

Row 27 SI 1, k1 tbl, 2/1 RPC, [k1, p1] 3 times, p1, k6, *[p1, k1] 3 times, p1, 2/1 LPC, k1 tbl, 2/1 RPC, [p1, k1] 3 times, p1, k6; rep from * to last 12 sts, [p1, k1] 3 times, p1, 2/1 LPC, k1 tbl, k1.

Row 28 SI 1, p3, [k1, p1] 4 times, *p6, [p1, k1] 4 times, p5, [k1, p1] 4 times; rep from * to last 18 sts, p6, [p1, k1] 4 times, p4.

Row 29 Purl.

Cont as desired.

cords

1x1 rib cord

▶ Cast on 6 sts.

Row 1 [K1, p1] 3 times, do not turn, slide sts to other end of needle.

Rep row 1 for desired length.

tube st

▶ Cast on 5 sts using straight needles.

Row 1 (RS) [K1, wyib sl 1 purlwise] twice, k1.

Row 2 (WS) [Wyif sl 1 purlwise, p1] twice, wyif sl 1 purlwise.

Rep rows 1 and 2 for desired length.

Notes

• When making cords, use two double-pointed needles or one short circular needle, unless otherwise indicated.

• The cords are made separately, then either sewn on or knit into the piece to form the edging.

6-st cable cord

▶ **2/2 LC** Sl 2 sts to cn and hold to front, k2, k2 from cn.

Cast on 6 sts.

Rows 1 to 5 Knit, do not turn, slide sts to other end of needle.

Row 6 K1, 2/2 LC, k1, do not turn, slide sts to other end of needle.

Rep rows 1 to 6 for desired length.

5-st cable cord

▶ **1/2 LC** Sl 1 st to cn and hold to front, k2, k1 from cn.

Cast on 5 sts.

Rows 1 to 4 Knit, do not turn, slide sts to other end of needle.

Row 5 K1, 1/2 LC, k1, do not turn, slide sts to other end of needle.

Rep rows 1 to 5 for desired length.

reverse stockinette st cord

▶ Cast on desired number of sts.

Row 1 Purl, do not turn, slide sts to other end of needle.

Rep row 1 for desired length.

eyelet cord

▶ Cast on 5 sts.

Rows 1, 2 and 4 Knit, do not turn, slide sts to other end of needle.

Row 3 K2, yo, k2tog, k1, do not turn, slide sts to other end of needle.

Rep rows 1 to 4 for desired length.

If desired, run a length of ribbon through eyelets.

yin & yang cord

▶ Cast on 7 sts.

Row 1 K4, wyif sl 3 purlwise, turn work.

Rep row 1 for desired length.

bobble cord

▶ **Make bobble (MB)** [K into front and back of st] twice—
4 sts; turn, p4, turn, k4, pass 2nd, 3rd and 4th sts, one at a
time, over first st.

Cast on 5 sts.

Rows 1 to 5 Knit, do not turn, slide sts to other end
of needle.

Row 6 K2, MB, k2, do not turn, slide sts to other end
of needle.

Rep rows 1 to 6 for desired length.

seed st cord

▶ Cast on an odd number of sts.

Row 1 K1, *p1, k1; rep from * to end, do not turn,
slide sts to other end of needle.

Row 2 P1, *k1, p1; rep from * to end, do not turn,
slide sts to other end of needle.

Rep rows 1 and 2 for desired length.

tube st with bobble

▸ **Make bobble (MB)** K into front, back, front, back and front of a st—5 sts; [turn, p5, turn, k5] twice, pass 2nd, 3rd, 4th and 5th sts, one at a time, over first st. Cast on 5 sts.

Rows 1, 3 and 5 (RS) [K1, wyib sl 1 purlwise] twice, k1.

Rows 2, 4 and 6 (WS) [Wyif sl 1 purlwise, p1] twice, wyif sl 1 purlwise.

Row 7 K1, wyib sl 1 purlwise, MB, wyib sl 1 purlwise, k1.

Row 8 Rep row 2.

Rep rows 1 to 8 for desired length.

banded cord

▸ Cast on 5 sts.

Rows 1 to 5 Knit, do not turn, slide sts to other end of needle.

Row 6 Purl, do not turn, slide sts to other end of needle.

Rep rows 1 to 6 for desired length.

basketweave cord

▸ Cast on desired number of sts.

Rows 1 to 5 Knit, do not turn, slide sts to other end of needle.

Rows 6 to 10 Purl, do not turn, slide sts to other end of needle.

Rep rows 1 to 10 for desired length.

scribble cord

▶ Make St st cord (see page 188) the desired number of sts and length. Form cord into a series of coiling loops approx 1 ½" (4cm) apart and sew in place along edge of knitted piece.

mock loops

▶ **Note** May also be used for button loops.
Make St st cord (see page 188) the desired number of sts and length. Sew cord in place along edge of knitted piece, forming 1" (2.5cm)-tall accordion loops approx ½" (1.25cm) apart.

fruit loops

▶ ▲ (multiple of 11 sts plus 8)
Invisibly cast on 3 sts. Work St st cord (see page 188) for 2½" (6.5cm). Remove waste yarn from invisible cast-on and place 3 sts onto same needle as first 3 sts. Place sts on spare needles. Rep for desired number of cords, placing all cords onto same needle.
Cast on a multiple of 11 sts plus 8 onto another needle. K 2 rows. Work in St st for 1½" (4cm), end with a WS row.

Join cords
Next row (RS) Hold needle with cords in front of and parallel to needle with St st, with needle point facing same direction, then k4 from back needle, *[k 1 cord st tog with 1 st on needle] 3 times, k5 from back needle, [k 1 cord st tog with 1 st on needle] 3 times; rep from *, end k 4 from back needle. Cont as desired.

braided cord

▶ Make three St st cords (see page 188) 1½ times the desired number of sts and finished length. Braid cords tog, securing ends.

beaded cord

▶ **Note** String beads onto yarn before knitting.

Cast on 5 sts.

Rows 1 to 3 Knit, do not turn, slide sts to other end of needle.

Row 4 K2, slide bead to needle, wyif sl 1 purlwise, k2, do not turn, slide sts to other end of needle.

Rep rows 1 to 4 for desired length.

knitted on cord

▶ (knit on after piece is knit)

Cast on 3 sts onto dpn.

Row 1 K2, sl 1, pick up and k1 st on edge, insert LH needle into fronts of first 2 sts on RH needle and k them tog, slide sts to other end of needle.

Rep row 1 for desired length.

knit-in cord edge on garter

▲ (cord is knit into the edge as piece is knit)

Cast on number of sts desired plus 3 to 5 cord sts.

Row 1 (RS) Knit.

Row 2 (WS) Wyif sl cord sts purlwise, bring yarn to back and k to end.

Rep rows 1 and 2 for desired length.

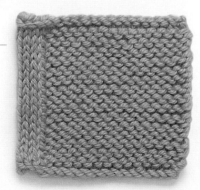

cord spokes

▲ (multiple of 8 sts plus 3 after cords are joined)

Cast on 5 sts. Work St st cord (see page 188) for 1" (2.5cm). Cut yarn. Sl sts onto spare needle. Rep for desired number of cords, placing cord sts onto same needle.

Join cords

Row 1 (RS) Single cast on 3 sts onto another needle then with same needle, *k5 from cord, single cast on 3 sts; rep from * to end. Cont in garter st (as shown) or desired pat.

seed st cord point

▲ (multiple of 10 sts plus 1 after cords are joined)

Cast on 5 sts.

Work Seed st cord (see page 52) for 1" (2.5cm), end with row 2.

Beg working back and forth in rows.

Row 1 (RS) [P1, k1] into first st, [p1, k1] twice.

Row 2 (WS) [P1, k1] into first st, [p1, k1] twice, p1.

Row 3 [K1, p1] into first st, [k1, p1] 3 times.

Row 4 [K1, p1] into first st, [k1, p1] 3 times, k1.

Row 5 [P1, k1] into first st, [p1, k1] 4 times.

Row 6 [P1, k1] into first st, [p1, k1] 4 times, p1—11 sts.

Cut yarn. Place sts onto a spare needle. Rep for desired number of cords, placing cord sts onto same needle. Leave yarn attached to last cord.

Join cords

Row 1 (RS) With another needle, work across all cord sts as foll: [P1, k1] 5 times, p2tog (joining first and 2nd cords), *[k1, p1] 4 times, k1, p2tog (joining 2 cords); rep from * until 10 sts of last cord rem, [k1, p1] 5 times.

Row 2 *P1, k1; rep from *, end p1. Rep row 2 until desired length.

Cont as desired.

2x3 rib with tied cord

▲ (multiple of 10 sts plus 3 after cords are joined)

Cast on 4 sts.

Work St st cord (see page 188) for desired length. [K2tog] twice—2 sts. Cut yarn. Sl sts onto spare needle. Rep for desired number of cords (an even number), placing cord sts onto same needle.

Join cords

Row 1 (RS) Single cast on 3 sts onto another needle, then with this same needle, *k2 from first cord, single cast on 3 sts; rep from * to end.

Row 2 (WS) K3, *p2, k3; rep from * to end.

Row 3 P3, *k2, p3; rep from * to end.

Rep rows 2 and 3 until desired length. Cont as desired.

Tie each pair of cords tog with knot at base of cords.

picot scallop cord

▶ ▲ (multiple of 5 sts plus 1 after sts are picked up along cord)

Cast on 3 sts. Work a multiple of 6 rows of St st cord (see page 188) until cord is as long as the desired width of finished piece.

Next row K3 cord sts tog, *single cast on 4 sts, skip 5 rows of cord and pick up and k1 st in next row of cord; rep from * to end. Cont in desired pat.

3-needle method ribbon cord scallop

▶ ▲ **Note** This edging is worked with straight needles along the cast-on or bound-off edge of a finished piece. The existing edge should have a multiple of 9 sts plus 3. With WS of finished piece facing, insert needle into loops along edge as foll: Insert needle into first 3 loops, *skip 6 loops, insert needle into next 3 loops; rep from * to end.

Edging

On another needle, cast on a multiple of 13 sts plus 3. K 4 rows, ending with a RS row. With a 3rd needle, join edging to completed piece as foll: Hold edging and piece with WS tog, needles parallel, and edging in back, k 1 st from front and back needles tog, *[k 1 st from front and back needles tog, pull first st over 2nd st] twice, bind off 10 sts from edging, k 1 st from front and back needles tog, pull first st over 2nd st; rep from *, end last rep [k 1 st from front and back needles tog, pull first st over 2nd st] 3 times.

accordion pleat cord

▶ ▲ (multiple of 5 sts plus 3 after cords are joined)

Using desired cord (see pages 58–63), make triple the amount of cord needed for width of piece. Form 1½" (4cm)-deep accordion pleats on a flat surface, with cast-on and bound-off ends pointing up. Insert a long needle into 2 sts on cast-on end, then into 2 horizontal bars in center of sts at top of each curve of cord (making sure that accordion pleats are the same length), end by inserting needle into 2 sts on bound-off end.

Next row (WS) Single cast on 3 sts onto another needle, *p2 cord sts, single cast-on 3 sts; rep from * to end.
Cont as desired.

cord fringe (attached)

▲ Make desired number of cords of any size and color (see pages 58-63). Bind off sts when cord is desired length, leaving a 4" (10cm) tail. Attach each cord to an edge by pulling tail through to back of work and tying it at back of piece. Cords can also be layered by pulling the tails through sts in middle of fabric.

frantic fringe cord I

▲ (multiple of 6 sts plus 3)

Make desired lengths and number of 3-st St st cords (see page 188). Place cords on spare needle. Cast onto another needle a multiple of 6 sts plus 3 and work in garter st for 1" (2.5cm), end with a WS row.

Join first row of cords

Next row (RS) Hold needle with cords in front of and parallel to needle with garter st, with needle point facing same direction, then *k3 from back needle, [k 1 cord st tog with 1 st on needle] 3 times; rep from *, end k3 from back needle. Work in garter st for 1" (2.5cm), end with a WS row.

Join 2nd row of cords

Next row (RS) K6, *[k 1 cord st tog with 1 st on needle] 3 times, k3; rep from *, end last rep k6.

K 1 row.

Cont as desired.

frantic fringe cord II

▲ Work **frantic fringe cord I** (see above) and add bobbles and fringe to ends of cords.

wrapped cord fringe

▲ (multiple of 7 sts plus 4 after cords are joined)

Wrap 3 (W3) [Wyif sl 3 sts purlwise, bring yarn to back, sl sts back to LH needle] 3 times, bring yarn to front again.

Make two 3-st St st cords (see page 188) 2" (5cm) long for each rep of pat. Cut yarn. Place cords onto spare needle.

Join cords

Row 1 (RS) *Single cast on 4 sts onto another needle, then with same needle, [k2tog] 3 times across cord sts; rep from *, end single cast on 4 sts.

Rows 2 and 4 *K4, p3; rep from *, end k4.

Row 3 *P4, W3; rep from *, end p4.

Row 5 *P4, k3; rep from *, end p4.

Rep rows 4 and 5 until desired length. Cont as desired.

cord fringe (knit in)

▲ Cast on 3 sts.

Work St st cord (see page 188) for desired length. Cut yarn. Sl sts onto spare needle. Rep for desired number of cords, placing cord sts onto same needle. Do not cut yarn on last cord.

Join cords

Next row (RS) With another needle, k across all cord sts. Cont in desired pat (swatch shows Seed st).

Cords may be knotted at ends.

cheery o's

▲ Make any cord (see pages 58–63) approx 2½" (6.5cm) long and attach to any background. Simply pull the cast-on and bind-off tails to back of piece, leaving one st in between the tails. Tie the tails tog to secure the cord.

looped basketweave cord

▶ ▲ (multiple of 15 sts plus 1 after cords are joined)

Invisibly cast on 5 sts. Work Basketweave cord (see page 53) for 3" (7.5cm). Cut yarn. Remove waste yarn from invisible cast-on and place 5 sts onto same needle with first 5 sts. Place sts on spare needle. Rep for desired number of cords, placing all cord sts onto same needle.

Join cords

Row 1 (RS) Single cast on 3 sts onto another needle, then with same needle, *k10 cord sts, single cast on 5 sts; rep from *, and last rep single cast on 3 sts.

Row 2 K3, *p10, k5; rep from *, end last rep k3.

Row 3 Knit.

Rep rows 2 and 3 until desired length. Cont as desired.

love knots

▶ ▲ (multiple of 8 sts after cords are joined)

Make two 4-st St st cords (see page 188) 2½" (6.5cm) long for each knot. Cut yarn. Place cords onto spare needle. Do not cut yarn on last cord.

Join cords

Row 1 (RS) Keeping RS of cords facing at all times, *cross first cord in front of 2nd cord, then bring cast-on edge of 2nd cord up in front of first cord and tuck it between the 2 cords and behind the first. K 4 sts of first cord at the same time catching in 4 of the cast-on sts of 2nd cord. Tuck cast-on edge of first cord behind sts of 2nd cord and k 4 sts of 2nd cord catching in 4 cast-on sts of first cord; rep from * to end.

Cont as desired.

seed st crossed loops

▶ ▲ (multiple of 10 sts plus 3 after cords are joined)

Work desired number of 5-st Seed st cords (see page 52), each 3½" (9cm) long.

Place all cord sts onto left needle, leaving yarn attached on last cord.

Join cords

Next row (RS) K5 sts of first cord, then *cross cast-on edge of first cord in front of and behind sts of 2nd cord, k5 sts of 2nd cord, at same time catching in 3 sts of cast-on edge of first cord; rep from *, end pick up and k3 sts from cast-on edge of last cord.

pretzel twist

▶ ▲ (multiple of 28 sts plus 3 after cords are joined)

Make two 5-st Seed st cords (see page 52) 4" (10cm) long for each 28-st rep of main pat. Cut yarn. Sl cord sts onto spare needle.

Join cords

Row 1 (RS) Single cast on 3 sts onto another needle, then *pick up and k3 sts along cast-on edge of first cord, single cast on 3 sts, k5 sts of cord, single cast on 3 sts, k5 sts of 2nd cord, single cast on 3 sts, loop the cast-on end of 2nd cord from back to front through loop of first cord, then pick up and k3 sts along cast-on edge of 2nd cord, single cast on 3 sts; rep from * to end.

Row 2 (WS) *K3, p3, [k3, p5] twice, k3, p3; rep from *, end k3.

Row 3 *P3, k3, [p3, k5] twice, p3, k3; rep from *, end p3.

Rep rows 2 and 3 until desired length.

Cont as desired.

seed st cord love knots

▶ ▲ (multiple of 12 sts plus 11 after cords are joined)

Make two 5-st Seed st cords (see page 52) 4" (10cm) long for each knot (if desired, use contrasting colors as shown here). Cut yarn. Place cords onto spare needle. Do not cut yarn on last cord.

Join cords

Row 1 (RS) Keeping RS of cords facing at all times, *cross first cord in front of 2nd cord, then bring cast-on edge of 2nd cord up in front of first cord and tuck it between the 2 cords and behind the first. Work Seed st over 5 sts of first cord at the same time catching in 2 of the cast-on sts of 2nd cord, single cast on 1 st, tuck cast-on edge of first cord behind sts of 2nd cord and work Seed st over 5 sts of 2nd cord catching in 2 cast-on sts of first cord, single cast on 1 st; rep from *, omitting last cast-on st on last rep.

Work 3 rows in Seed st.

Cont as desired.

half moon scallop cord

▶ ▲ (multiple of 13 sts plus 1 after cords are joined)
Invisibly cast on 3 sts. Work St st cord (see page 188)
for 3½" (9cm). Cut yarn. Remove waste yarn from invisible cast-on and place 3 sts onto same needle with first
3 sts. Place sts on spare needles. Rep for desired number (and color sequence) of cords, placing all cord sts
onto same needle.

Join cords

Row 1 (RS) Single cast on 1 st onto another needle, then
with this same needle, *k3 cord sts, single cast on 6 sts,
k3 cast-on sts of same cord, single cast on 1 st; rep
from * to end. Cont in desired pat.

chaplet loop with garter ridges

▶ Cast on 40 sts using straight
needles.

Row 1 (RS) K to last 3 sts, yo, k2tog, k1.

Row 2 K3, p to end.

Row 3 Bind off 28 sts, k to last 3 sts,
yo, k2tog, k1—12 sts.

Rows 4 and 8 Knit.

Rows 5, 7, 9 and 11 K9, yo, k2tog, k1.

Rows 6 and 10 K3, p9.

Row 12 K12, cast on 28 sts—40 sts.

Row 13 K to last 3 sts, yo, k2tog, k1.

Row 14 K3, p to end.

Row 15 Bind off 28 sts, k to last 3 sts,
yo, k2tog, k1—12 sts.

Row 16 Knit.

Rows 17 and 19 K9, yo, k2tog, k1.

Row 18 K3, p9.

Row 20 K12, turn up the first unat-
tached narrow strip of knitting and k
into first bound-off st.

Row 21 K2tog, k8, yo, k2tog, k1.

Row 22 K3, p9, p last cast-on st of
same strip.

Row 23 Rep row 21.

Rep rows 12 to 23 for desired length
(on last rep, omit 28 cast-on sts on
row 12).

hoop la

▶ ▲ (multiple of 13 sts plus 4 after cords are joined)

First Layer

Invisibly cast on 4 sts. Work St st cord (see page 188) for approx 4" (10cm). Cut yarn. Remove waste yarn from invisible cast-on and place 4 sts onto same needle with first 4 sts. Place sts on spare needles. Rep for desired number of cords, placing all cord sts onto same needle.

Join cords

Row 1 (RS) Single cast on 2 sts onto another needle, then with this same needle, *k4 cord sts, single cast on 5 sts, k4 cast-on sts of same cord; rep from *, end single cast on 2 sts. Beg with a purl row, work in St st for 1" (2.5cm), end with a WS row. Do not cut yarn.

2nd Layer

Work cords same as above, placing them onto a spare needle.

Join cords

Hold needle with 2nd layer cords parallel to and in front of needle with first layer cords with needle points facing same direction. Using a 3rd needle, k2 from back needle, *[k1 cord st of front needle tog with 1 st of back needle] 4 times, k5 from back needle, [k1 cord st of front needle tog with 1 st of back needle] 4 times; rep from *, end k2 from back needle. Cont as desired.

multi length loopy cords

▶ ▲ (multiple of 16 sts after cords are joined)

Invisibly cast on 4 sts. Work St st cord (see page 188) for desired length. Work another cord and place those sts on same needle as first cord. Remove waste yarn from invisible cast-on of first cord and place 4 sts on needle to left of 2nd cord. Remove waste yarn from cast-on of 2nd cord and place 4 sts on needle to left of cast-on sts of first cord—one loopy cord complete. Place loopy cord onto spare needle. Make desired number of loopy cords, placing them on same needle (do not cut yarn on last cord).

Join cords

Knit across all cord sts.

Cont as desired.

cord n' cable

▶ ▲ **4/4 LC** Sl 4 sts to cn and hold to front, k4, k4 from cn. (multiple of 12 sts plus 4 after cords are joined)

Invisibly cast on 4 sts. Work St st cord (see page 188) for 2½" (6.5cm). Cut yarn. Remove waste yarn from invisible cast-on and place 4 sts onto same needle with first 4 sts. Place sts on spare needle. Rep for desired number of cords, placing all cord sts onto same needle.

Join cords

Row 1 (RS) Single cast on 4 sts onto another needle, then with same needle, *k 4 cord sts, then k 4 cast-on sts from same cord, single cast on 4 sts; rep from * to end.

Rows 2, 4, 6, 8 and 10 (WS) *K4, p8; rep from *, end k4.

Rows 3, 7, 9 and **11** *P4, k8; rep from *, end p4.

Row 5 *P4, 4/4 LC; rep from *, end p4.

Rep rows 2 to 11 until desired length, end with row 6.

Cont as desired.

cable key chain

▶ ▲ **2/2 LC** Sl 2 sts to cn and hold to front, k2, k2 from cn. (multiple of 8 sts plus 4 after cords are joined)

Invisibly cast on 4 sts. Work St st cord (see page 188) for 2 ½" (6.5cm). Cut yarn. Remove waste yarn from invisible cast-on and place 4 sts onto same needle with first 4 sts. Place sts on spare needle. Rep for desired number of cords, placing all cord sts onto same needle.

Join cords

Row 1 (RS) *Single cast on 4 sts onto another needle, then with same needle, [k2tog] 4 times from cord; rep from *, end single cast on 4 sts.

Rows 2 and 4 *K4, p4; rep from *, end k4.

Row 3 *P4, k4; rep from *, end p4.

Row 5 *P4, 2/2 LC; rep from *, end p4.

Rep rows 2 to 5 until desired length.

Cont as desired.

bell pull loops

▶ ▲ **2/2 RPC** Sl 2 sts to cn and hold to back, k2, p2 from cn.

2/2 LPC Sl 2 sts to cn and hold to front, p2, k2 from cn.

3/2 RPC Sl 2 sts to cn and hold to back, k3, p2 from cn.

3/2 LPC Sl 3 sts to cn and hold to front, p2, k3 from cn.

Wrap 5 (W5) [Wyif sl 5 sts purlwise, bring yarn to back, sl sts back to LH needle] 3 times, bring yarn to front again.

(multiple of 18 sts plus 5 after cords are joined)

Make three 3-st St st cords (see page 188) 2½" (6.5cm) long for each rep of pat. Cut yarn. Place cords onto spare needle.

Join cords

Row 1 (RS) Single cast on 5 sts onto another needle, then with same needle, *[k3 cord sts, single cast on 2 sts] twice, k3 cord sts, single cast on 5 sts; rep from * to end.

Rows 2 and 4 K5, *[p3, k2] twice, p3, k5; rep from * to end.

Row 3 P5, *[k3, p2] twice, k3, p5; rep from * to end.

Row 5 P5, *3/2 LPC, k3, 3/2 RPC, p5; rep from * to end.

Rows 6, 8 and 10 K7, *p9, k9; rep from *, end last rep k7.

Rows 7 and 9 P7, *k9, p9; rep from *, end last rep p7.

Row 11 P7, *2/2 LPC, k1, 2/2 RPC, p9; rep from *, end last rep p7.

Rows 12 and 14 K9, *p5, k13; rep from *, end last rep k9.

Row 13 P9, *k5, p13; rep from *, end last rep p9.

Row 15 P9, *W5, p13; rep from *, end last rep p9.

Rows 16, 18 and 20 Rep row 12.

Rows 17 and 19 Rep row 13.

Cont as desired.

Sew cast-on edges of cords to back of work to form loops.

loop de loops

▶ ▲ (multiple of 20 sts plus 2 after cords are joined)

Invisibly cast on 3 sts. Work St st cord (see page 188) for 2½" (6.5cm). Cut yarn. Remove waste yarn from invisible cast-on and place 3 sts onto same needle with first 3 sts. Invisibly cast on 3 sts and work another St st cord for 5" (12.5cm). Cut yarn. Sl sts onto right-hand end of same needle as smaller cord. Remove waste yarn from invisible cast-on and place 3 sts onto left-hand end of same needle—one loop de loop completed. Rep for desired number of loop de loops, placing all cord sts onto same needle.

Join cords

Row 1 (RS) Single cast on 2 sts onto another needle, *k3 cord sts, single cast on 2 sts; rep from * to end.

Row 2 *K2, p3; rep from *, end k2.

Row 3 *P2, k3; rep from *, end p2.

Rep rows 2 and 3 until desired length.

Cont as desired.

double orbs

▶ ▲ (multiple of 12 sts plus 6 after cords are joined, dec'd to a multiple of 9 sts plus 6)

With main color yarn, invisibly cast on 3 sts. Work St st cord (see page 188) for 2½" (6.5cm). Cut yarn. Remove waste yarn from invisible cast-on and place 3 sts onto same needle with first 3 sts. Using a contrasting color yarn, invisibly cast on 3 sts and work another St st cord for 3½" (9cm). Cut yarn. Sl sts onto right-hand end of same needle as smaller cord. Remove waste yarn from invisible cast on and place 3 sts onto left-hand end of same needle—one double orb completed. Place sts on spare needle.

Rep for desired number of double orbs, placing all cord sts onto same needle.

Join cords

Row 1 (RS) With main color, single cast on 6 sts onto another needle, *[k2tog] 6 times across 12 sts of first double orb, single cast on 6 sts; rep from * to end.

Row 2 *K6, [p2tog] 3 times; rep from *, end k6.

Row 3 *P6, k3; rep from *, end p6.

Row 4 *K6, p3; rep from *, end k6.

Rep rows 3 and 4 until desired length. Cont as desired.

herringbone

▶ ▲ (multiple of 32 sts plus 1 after cords are joined)

Make one 4-st St st cord (see page 188) 3½" (9cm) long using invisible cast on and two cords 1½" (4cm) long using any cast-on for every 32-st rep of pat. Make one more 3 ½" (9cm) long cord for last half rep and two more 1½" (4cm) long cords for each 1/4 rep at side edges. Cut yarn for each cord. Place cords onto spare needle in correct sequence for pat (remove waste yarn from invisible cast-ons of longer cords and place these sts on needle to left of cord sts).

Join cords

Row 1 (RS) Single cast on 3 sts onto another needle, then with same needle, [k2tog] twice from first shorter cord, single cast on 3 sts, *single cast on 4 sts, [k2tog] twice from next longer cord, single cast on 5 sts, [k2tog] twice from cast-on sts of same cord, single cast on 7 sts, [k2tog] twice from next shorter cord, single cast on 5 sts, [k2tog] twice from next shorter cord, single cast on 3 sts; rep from * to last longer cord, single cast on 4 sts, [k2tog] twice from longer cord, single cast on 5 sts, [k2tog] twice from cast-on sts of same cord, single cast on 7 sts, [k2tog] twice from last shorter cord, single cast on 3 sts.

Row 2 (WS) *P1, k2, p2, k2, p3, k2, p2, k2; rep from *, end p1.

Row 3 K2tog, *p1, k2, p2, [k1, yo] twice, k1, p2, k2, p1, S2KP2; rep from *, end last rep ssk, instead of S2KP2.

Row 4 *P1, k1, p2, k2, p5, k2, p2, k1; rep from *, end p1.

Row 5 K2tog, *k2, p2, k2, yo, k1, yo, k2, p2, k2, S2KP2; rep from *, end last rep ssk, instead of S2KP2.

Row 6 *P3, k2, p7, k2, p2; rep from *, end last rep p3.

Row 7 K2tog, *k1, p2, k2, p1, yo, k1, yo, p1, k2, p2, k1, S2KP2; rep from *, end last rep ssk, instead of S2KP2.

Row 8 *P2, k2, p2, k1, p3, k1, p2, k2, p1; rep from *, end last rep p2.

Row 9 K2tog, *p2, k2, p2, yo, k1, yo, p2, k2, p2, S2KP2; rep from *, end last rep ssk, instead of S2KP2.

Rep rows 2 to 9 until desired length, end with row 8.

Cont as desired.

Sew cast-on ends of shorter cords to WS of work, forming teardrops.

aqueduct

▶ ▲ **2/1 RC** Sl 1 st to cn and hold to back, k2, k1 from cn.

2/1 LC Sl 2 sts to cn and hold to front, k1, k2 from cn.

2/1 RPC Sl 1 st to cn and hold to back, k2, p1 from cn.

2/1 LPC Sl 2 sts to cn and hold to front, p1, k2 from cn.

2/2 RC Sl 2 sts to cn and hold to back, k2, k2 from cn.

2/2 LC Sl 2 sts to cn and hold to front, k2, k2 from cn.

2/2 RPC Sl 2 sts to cn and hold to back, k2, p2 from cn.

2/2 LPC Sl 2 sts to cn and hold to front, p2, k2 from cn.

(multiple of 11 sts plus 2 after cords are joined, inc'd to 13 sts plus 2, dec'd to 9 sts plus 2)

Note If desired, omit last cord altogether (cast on these three sts instead) and graft 3 cast-on sts of 2nd to last cord to these 3 sts. Make one 5-st St st cord (see page 188) 3" (7.5cm) long for each rep of main pat. Cut yarn. Place cords onto spare needle.

Join cords

Row 1 (RS) Single cast on 5 sts onto another needle, then with this same needle, *k2tog, k1, k2tog from first cord, single cast on 8 sts; rep from *, end last rep single cast on 5 sts.

Rows 2, 4, 6, 8 and 10 K5, *p3, k8; rep from *, end last rep k5.

Rows 3, 5, 7 and 9 P5, *k1, wyib sl 1 purlwise, k1, p8; rep from *, end last rep p5.

Row 11 P5, *k 1 into back and front of next st, then insert tip of LH needle behind the vertical strand that runs downward from between the 2 sts just made, and k this strand tbl (2 sts inc'd), k1, p8; rep from *, end last rep p5.

Row 12 K5, *p2, k1, p2, k8; rep from *, end last rep k5.

Row 13 P4, *2/1 RC, p1, 2/1 LC, p6; rep from *, end last rep p4.

Row 14 K4, *p2, p1 tbl, k1, p1 tbl, p2, k6; rep from *, end last rep k4.

Row 15 P3, *2/1 RPC, k1 tbl, p1, k1 tbl, 2/1 LPC, p4; rep from *, end last rep p3.

Row 16 K3, *p2, [k1, p1 tbl] twice, k1, p2, k4; rep from *, end last rep k3.

Row 17 P1, *2/2 RC, [p1, k1 tbl] twice, p1, 2/2 LC; rep from *, end p1.

Rows 18 and 20 K1, *p2, [k1, p1 tbl] 4 times, k1, p2; rep from *, end k1.

Row 19 P1, k2, *[p1, k1 tbl] 4 times, p1, 2/2 RC; rep from *, end last rep k2, p1 (instead of 2/2 RC).

Row 21 P1, *2/2 LPC, [p1, k1 tbl] twice, p1, 2/2 RPC; rep from *, end p1.

Row 22 K3, *p2, [k1, p1 tbl] twice, k1, p2, k4; rep from *, end last rep k3.

Row 23 P3, *2/2 LPC, p1, 2/2 RPC, p4; rep from *, end last rep p3.

Row 24 K5, *p2tog, p3tog tbl, pass p2tog st over p3tog tbl st, k8; rep from *, end last rep k5.

Cont as desired. Sew cast-on edge of each cord in back of cord to its left to form scallops.

deco lozenges

▶ ▲ **Wrap 3 (W3)** Wyib sl 3 sts purlwise, pass yarn to front, sl same 3 sts back to LH needle, pass yarn to back, k3.

Make bobble (MB) [K1, yo, k1, yo, k1] into same st, turn, p5, turn, k5, turn, p2tog, p1, p2tog, turn, SK2P.

2/1 RC Sl 1 st to cn and hold to back, k2, k1 from cn.

2/1 LC Sl 2 sts to cn and hold to front, k1, k2 from cn.

(multiple of 14 sts plus 3 after cords are joined, inc'd to a multiple of 16 sts plus 3)

Make one 5-st St st (see page 188) cord 2½" (6.5cm) long for each rep (and half rep) of main pat. Cut yarn. Place cords onto spare needle. Do not cut yarn on last cord.

Join cords

Row 1 (RS) *K2tog, k1, k2tog from first cord, single cast on 11 sts; rep from *, end k2tog, k1, k2tog from last cord.

Rows 2, 4, 6, 8 and 10 *P3, k5, p1, k5; rep from *, end p3.

Row 3 *W3, p5, k1 tbl, p5; rep from *, end W3.

Rows 5, 7 and 9 *K3, p5, k1 tbl, p5; rep from *, end k3.

Row 11 K1, *k1, M1, k1, p5, MB, p5, k1, M1; rep from *, end k2.

Row 12 P4, *k11, p5; rep from *, end last rep p4.

Row 13 K1, p1, *2/1 LC, p9, 2/1 RC, p1; rep from *, end k1.

Row 14 *P1, k1, p3, k9, p2; rep from *, end p1, k1, p1.

Row 15 *P1, k1, p1, 2/1 LC, p7, 2/1 RC; rep from *, end p1, k1, p1.

Row 16 *K1, p1, k1, p3, k7, p3; rep from *, end k1, p1, k1.

Row 17 K1, p1, k1, *p1, 2/1 LC, p5, 2/1 RC, [p1, k1] twice; rep from * to end.

Row 18 P1, k1, p1, *k1, p3, k5, p3, [k1, p1] twice; rep from * to end.

Row 19 P1, k1, p1, *k1, p1, 2/1 LC, p3, 2/1 RC, [p1, k1] twice, p1; rep from * to end.

Row 20 K1, p1, k1, *p1, k1, p3, k3, p3, [k1, p1] twice, k1; rep from * to end.

Row 21 K1, p1, k1, *p1, k1, p1, 2/1 LC, p1, 2/1 RC, [p1, k1] 3 times; rep from * to end.

Row 22 *[P1, k1] 3 times, p2, wyif sl 1, p2tog tbl, psso, p2, k1, p1, k1; rep from *, end p1, k1, p1.

Row 23 P1, k1 tbl, *p5, W3, p5, k1 tbl; rep from *, end p1.

Rows 24, 26, 28 and 30 K1, *p1, k5, p3, k5; rep from *, end p1, k1.

Rows 25, 27 and 29 P1, *k1 tbl, p5, k3, p5; rep from *, end k1 tbl, p1.

Row 31 P1, *MB, p5, [k1, M1] twice, k1, p5; rep from *, end MB, p1.

Row 32 K7, *p5, k11; rep from *, end last rep k7.

Row 33 P6, *2/1 RC, p1, 2/1 LC, p9; rep from *, end last rep p6.

Row 34 K6, *p3, k1, p3, k9; rep from *, end last rep k6.

Row 35 P5, *2/1 RC, p1, k1, p1, 2/1 LC, p7; rep from *, end last rep p5.

Row 36 K5, *p3, k1, p1, k1, p3, k7; rep from *, end last rep k5.

Cont as desired.

Sew cast-on ends of cords to back of work, forming teardrops.

persian lace cord drops

▶ ▲ (multiple of 8 sts plus 2)

Make one 4-st St st cord (see page 188) 1¼" (3cm) long for each rep of pat. Cut yarn. Place cords onto spare needle.

Join cords

Row 1 (RS) Single cast on 4 sts onto another needle, then with same needle, *[k2tog] twice from first cord, single cast on 6 sts; rep from *, end last rep single cast on 4 sts.

Rows 2 and 4 (WS) K4, *p2, k6; rep from *, end last rep k4.

Row 3 K1, p3, *k2, p6; rep from *, end last rep p3, k1.

Row 5 K1, p2, * k2tog, yo, ssk, p4; rep from *, end last rep p2, k1.

Row 6 K3, *p1, p into front and back of yo, p1, k4; rep from *, end last rep k3.

Row 7 K1, p1, *k2tog, yo, k2, yo, ssk, p2; rep from *, end last rep p1, k1.

Row 8 K2, *p6, k2; rep from * to end.

Row 9 K1, *[k2tog, yo] twice, ssk, yo, ssk; rep from *, end k1.

Row 10 K1, p3, *p into front and back of yo, p6; rep from *, end last rep p3, k1.

Row 11 K1, *[yo, ssk] twice, k2tog, yo, k2tog; rep from *, end yo, k1.

Row 12 K1, k yo tbl, p6, *p into front and back of yo, p6; rep from *, end k yo tbl, k1.

Row 13 K1, p1, *yo, SK2P, yo, k3tog, yo, p2; rep from *, end last rep p1, k1.

Row 14 K2, *k yo tbl, p1, p into front and back of yo, p1, k yo tbl, k2; rep from * to end.

Row 15 K1, p2, *yo, ssk, k2tog, yo, p4; rep from *, end last rep p2, k1.

Row 16 K3, *k yo tbl, p2, k yo tbl, k4; rep from *, end last rep k3.

Rows 17 and 18 Rep rows 3 and 4.

Cont as desired.

balloon border

▶ ▲ (multiple of 11 sts plus 4 after cords are joined)

1/1 RC Sl 1 st to cn and hold to back, k1, k1 from cn.

1/1 LC Sl 1 st to cn and hold to front, k1, k1 from cn.

Cast on 5 sts.

Work St st cord (see page 188) for 3" (7.5cm). Cut yarn. Sl sts onto spare needle.

Rep for desired number of cords, placing cord sts onto same needle.

Join cords

Row 1 (RS) Single cast on 6 sts onto another needle, then with same needle, *k2tog, k1, k2tog from first cord, single cast on 8 sts; rep from *, end last rep cast on 6 sts. Cont as desired. If desired, knot ends of cords.

Rows 2 and 4 K6, *p1, p1 tbl, p1, k8; rep from *, end last rep k6.

Row 3 P6, *k1, k1 tbl, k1, p8; rep from *, end last rep p6.

Row 5 P5, *1/1 RC, k1 tbl, 1/1 LC, p6; rep from *, end last rep p5.

Row 6 K5, *p1, k1, p1 tbl, k1, p1, k6; rep from *, end last rep k5.

Row 7 P4, *1/1 RC, p1, k1 tbl, p1, 1/1 LC, p4; rep from * to end.

Row 8 K4, *p1, k2, p1 tbl, k2, p1, k4; rep from * to end.

Row 9 P3, *1/1 RC, p2, [k1, yo, k1, yo, k1] into next st, p2, 1/1 LC, p2; rep from *, end last rep p3.

Row 10 P1, k2, *p1, k3, p5, k3, p1, k2; rep from *, end p1.

Row 11 *1/1 LC, 1/1 RC, p3, k1, M1, k3, M1, k1, p3; rep from *, end 1/1 LC, 1/1 RC.

Row 12 K1, *p2, k4, p7, k4; rep from *, end p2, k1.

Row 13 P1, *1/1 LC, p4, k1, M1, k5, M1, k1, p4; rep from * end 1/1 RC, p1.

Row 14 K1, *p2, k4, p9, k4; rep from *, end p2, k1.

Row 15 *1/1 RC, 1/1 LC, p3, ssk, k5, k2tog, p3; rep from *, end 1/1 RC, 1/1 LC.

Row 16 *P1, k2, p1, k3, p2tog, p3, ssp, k3; rep from *, end p1, k2, p1.

Row 17 P3, *1/1 LC, p2, ssk, k1, k2tog, p2, 1/1 RC, p2; rep from *, end last rep p3.

Row 18 *K4, p1, k2, p3tog, k2, p1; rep from *, end k4.

Row 19 *P4, 1/1 LC, p3, 1/1 RC; rep from *, end p4.

Row 20 K5, *p1, k3, p1, k6; rep from *, end last rep k5.

Row 21 P5, *1/1 LC, p1, 1/1 RC, p6; rep from *, end last rep p5.

Row 22 K6, *p1, k1, p1, k8; rep from *, end last rep k6.

Row 23 P6, *k3, p8; rep from *, end last rep p6.

Cont as desired.

grillwork lattice

▶ ▲ **2/2 RC** Sl 2 sts to cn and hold to back, k2, k2 from cn.

2/2 LC Sl 2 sts to cn and hold to front, k2, k2 from cn.

2/2 RPC Sl 2 sts to cn and hold to back, k2, p2 from cn.

2/2 LPC Sl 2 sts to cn and hold to front, p2, k2 from cn.

(multiple of 8 sts after cords are joined)

Make one 5-st Cable cord (see page 51) 1½" (4cm) long for each rep of pat. Cut yarn. Place cords onto spare needle.

Join cords

Row 1 (RS) Single cast on 2 sts onto another needle, then with same needle, *k3, k2tog from cord, single cast on 4 sts; rep from *, end last rep single cast on 2 sts.

Rows 2, 4, 6, 8, 10 and 12 (WS) K2, *p4, k4; rep from *, end last rep k2.

Rows 3, 7 and 11 P2, *2/2 RC, p4; rep from *, end last rep p2.

Rows 5 and 9 P2, *k4, p4; rep from *, end last rep p2.

Row 13 P2, k2, *2/2 LPC, 2/2 RPC; rep from *, end k2, p2.

Rows 14 and 16 K2, p2, k2, *p4, k4; rep from * to last 10 sts, p4, k2, p2, k2.

Row 15 P2, k2, p2, *2/2 LC, p4; rep from * to last 10 sts, 2/2 LC, p2, k2, p2.

Row 17 P2, k2, *2/2 RPC, 2/2 LPC; rep from *, end k2, p2.

Rows 18 and 20 K2, *p4, k4; rep from *, end last rep k2.

Row 19 P2, *2/2 RC, p4; rep from *, end last rep p2.

Cont as desired.

orb knots

▶ ▲ **1/1 LC** Sl 1 st to cn and hold to front, k1, k1 from cn.

1/1 RPC Sl 1 st to cn and hold to back, k1, p1 from cn.

1/1 LPC Sl 1 st to cn and hold to front, p1, k1 from cn.

2/1 RC Sl 1 st to cn and hold to back, k2, k1 from cn.

2/1 RPC Sl 1 st to cn and hold to back, k2, p1 from cn.

2/1 LPC Sl 2 sts to cn and hold to front, p1, k2 from cn.

2/2 LC Sl 2 sts to cn and hold to front, k2, k2 from cn.

2/2 RPC Sl 2 sts to cn and hold to back, k2, p2 from cn.

2/2 LPC Sl 2 sts to cn and hold to front, p2, k2 from cn.

(multiple of 15 sts plus 10 after cords are joined)

Make two 5-st St st cords (see page 188) 2" (5cm) long for each rep of pat. Cut yarn. Place cords onto spare needle.

Join cords

Row 1 (RS) Single cast on 7 sts onto another needle, then with same needle, *k2tog, k1, k2tog from first cord, single cast on 5 sts, k2tog, k1, k2tog from 2nd cord, single cast on 4 sts; rep from *, end last rep single cast on 7 sts.

Rows 2 and 4 K1, p2, k4, *p3, k5, p3, k4; rep from *, end p2, k1.

Row 3 P1, k2, *p4, 2/1 RC, p5, 2/1 RC; rep from *, end p4, k2, p1.

Row 5 P1, *2/2 LPC, 2/2 RPC, 1/1 LPC, p3, 1/1 RPC; rep from * to last 9 sts, 2/2 LPC, 2/2 RPC, p1.

Row 6 K3, p4, *[k3, p1] twice, k3, p4; rep from *, end k3.

Row 7 P3, *2/2 LC, p3, 1/1 LPC, p1, 1/1 RPC, p3; rep from *, end 2/2 LC, p3.

Row 8 K3, p4, *k4, p1, k1, p1, k4, p4; rep from *, end k3.

Row 9 P3, *k4, p4, SK2P, p4; rep from *, end k4, p3.

Rows 10 and 12 K3, p4, *k4, p1, k4, p4; rep from *, end k3.

Row 11 P3, *k4, p4, k1, p4; rep from *, end k4, p3.

Row 13 K into front and back of first st, p2, *ssk, k2tog, p4, [k into back, front, back] of next st, p4; rep from * to last 7 sts, ssk, k2tog, p2, k into front and back of last st.

Row 14 K4, p2, k4, *p3, k4, p2, k4; rep from * to end.

Row 15 P4, 1/1 LC, p4, *k1, [k into back, front, back] of next st, k1, p4, 1/1 LC, p4; rep from * to end.

Row 16 *[K4, p2] twice, k1, p2; rep from * to last 10 sts, k4, p2, k4.

Row 17 P3, *1/1 RPC, 1/1 LPC, p2, 2/1 RPC, p1, 2/1 LPC, p2; rep from * to last 7 sts, 1/1 RPC, 1/1 LPC, p3.

Row 18 K3, [p1, k2] twice, *p2, k3, p2, k2, [p1, k2] twice; rep from *, end k1.

Row 19 P2, 1/1 RPC, p2, 1/1 LPC, *2/1 RPC, p3, 2/1 LPC, 1/1 RPC, p2, 1/1 LPC; rep from *, end p2.

Row 20 K2, p1, k4, *p3, k5, p3, k4; rep from *, end p1, k2.

Cont as desired.

Sew cast-on edge of cords to back of work, creating teardrops.

interlocks

▶ ▲ **2/2 RC** Sl 2 sts to cn and hold to back, k2, k2 from cn.

2/2 LC Sl 2 sts to cn and hold to front, k2, k2 from cn.

2/2 RPC Sl 2 sts to cn and hold to back, k2, p2 from cn.

2/2 LPC Sl 2 sts to cn and hold to front, p2, k2 from cn.

(multiple of 13 sts plus 1 after cords are joined, inc'd to a multiple of 17 sts plus 1)

Invisibly cast on 4 sts. Work St st cord (see page 188) for 2 ½" (6.5cm). Cut yarn. Remove waste yarn from invisible cast-on and place 4 sts onto same needle with first 4 sts. Place sts on spare needle. Rep for desired number of cords, placing cord sts onto same needle.

Join cords

Row 1 (RS) Single cast on 5 sts onto another needle, then with same needle, *[k2tog] 4 times from cord, single cast on 9 sts; rep from *, end last rep single cast on 5 sts.

Row 2 K5, *p4, k9; rep from *, end last rep k5.

Row 3 K into back and front of first st, M1, p4, *2/2 RC, p4, M1, k into back and front of next st, then insert tip of LH needle behind the vertical strand that runs downward from between the 2 sts just made, and k this strand tbl (2 sts inc'd), M1, p4; rep from * to last 9 sts, 2/2 RC, p4, M1, k into back and front of last st.

Row 4 *K1, p2, k4, p4, k4, p2; rep from *, end k1.

Row 5 P1, *[2/2 LPC, 2/2 RPC] twice, p1; rep from * to end.

Rows 6 and 8 K1, *k2, p4, k4, p4, k3; rep from * to end.

Row 7 P1, *p2, 2/2 LC, p4, 2/2 LC, p3; rep from * to end.

Row 9 P1, *[2/2 RPC, 2/2 LPC] twice, p1; rep from * to end.

Row 10 P3tog tbl, k4, p4, k4, *p2tog, p3tog tbl, pass p2tog st over p3tog tbl st, k4, p4, k4; rep from * to last 3 sts, wyif sl 1 purlwise, p2tog tbl, psso.

Row 11 P5, *2/2 LC, p9; rep from *, end last rep p5.

Row 12 K5, *p4, k9; rep from *, end last rep k5.

Row 13 P3, *2/2 RPC, 2/2 LPC, p5; rep from *, end last rep p3.

Row 14 K1, *k2, p2, k4, p2, k3; rep from * to end.

Row 15 P3, *2/2 LPC, 2/2 RPC, p5; rep from *, end last rep p3.

Rep rows 2 to 10 once more.

Cont as desired.

chain link knots

▲ **2/1 RPC** Sl 1 st to cn and hold to back, k2, p1 from cn.

2/1 LPC Sl 2 sts to cn and hold to front, p1, k2 from cn.

2/2 LC Sl 2 sts to cn and hold to front, k2, k2 from cn.

2/2 RPC Sl 2 sts to cn and hold to back, k2, p2 from cn.

2/2 LPC Sl 2 sts to cn and hold to front, p2, k2 from cn.

2/3 RPC Sl 3 sts to cn and hold to back, k2, p3 from cn.

2/3 LPC Sl 2 sts to cn and hold to front, p3, k2 from cn.

(multiple of 7 sts plus 3, inc'd to a multiple of 11 sts plus 10, dec'd to 7 sts plus 3)

Make one 3-st St st cord (see page 188) 2" (5cm) long for every rep of main pat. Tie cord into a knot and sew bound-off edge to cast-on edge.

Rows 1 and 3 (RS) P8, *k1 tbl, p6; rep from *, end last rep p8.

Rows 2 and 4 K8, *p1, k6; rep from *, end last rep k8.

Row 5 P8, *M1, [k1, p1, k1] into next st, M1, p6; rep from *, end last rep p8.

Row 6 K8, *p2, k1, p2, k6; rep from *, end last rep k8.

Row 7 P5, *2/3 RPC, p1, 2/3 LPC; rep from *, end p5.

Row 8 K5, p2, k7, *p4, k7; rep from * to last 7 sts, p2, k5.

Row 9 P3, 2/2 RPC, p7, *2/2 LC, p7; rep from * to last 7 sts, 2/2 LPC, p3.

Row 10 K3, p2, k9, *p4, k7; rep from * to last 7 sts, k2, p2, k3.

Row 11 P2, 2/1 RPC, p8, *2/1 RPC, 2/1 LPC, p5; rep from * to last 8 sts, p3, 2/1 LPC, p2.

Rows 12 and 14 K2, p2, k9, *p2, k2, p2, k5; rep from * to last 8 sts, k4, p2, k2.

Row 13 P2, k2, p9, *k2, p2, k2, p5; rep from * to last 8 sts, p4, k2, p2.

Row 15 P2, 2/1 LPC, p8, *2/1 LPC, 2/1 RPC, p5; rep from * to last 8 sts, p3, 2/1 RPC, p2.

Row 16 Rep row 10.

Row 17 P3, 2/2 LPC, p7, *2/2 LC, p7; rep from * to last 7 sts, 2/2 RPC, p3.

Row 18 Rep row 8.

Row 19 P5, *2/3 LPC, p1, 2/3 RPC; rep from *, end p5.

Row 20 K8, *p2tog, p3tog tbl, pass p2tog st over p3tog tbl st, k6; rep from *, end last rep k8.

Cont as desired.

Make cord knots and attach to every spoke of chain link along lower edge.

branching rib cords

▶ ▲ (multiple of 8 sts plus 4 after cords are joined)

1/1 RC Sl 1 st to cn and hold to back, k1, k1 from cn.

1/1 LC Sl 1 st to cn and hold to front, k1, k1 from cn.

1/1 RPC Sl 1 st to cn and hold to back, k1, p1 from cn.

1/1 LPC Sl 1 st to cn and hold to front, p1, k1 from cn.

Make one 5-st St st cord (see page 188) 1¼" (3cm) long for each rep (or half rep) of pat. Cut yarn. Place cords onto spare needle. Do not cut yarn on last cord.

Join cords

Row 1 (RS) *K2tog, k1, k2tog from first cord, single cast on 5 sts; rep from *, end last rep, single cast on 1 st.

Rows 2, 4 and 6 (WS) K1, p3, *k5, p3; rep from * to end.

Row 3 *1/1 LC, k1, p5; rep from *, end 1/1 LC, k1, p1.

Row 5 *K1, 1/1 LC, p5; rep from *, end k1, 1/1 LC, p1.

Row 7 P1, k2, *p4, 1/1 RPC, k2; rep from *, end p1.

Row 8 K1, *p2, k1, p1, k4; rep from *, end p2, k1.

Row 9 P1, k2, *p3, 1/1 RPC, p1, k2; rep from *, end p1.

Row 10 K1, *p2, k2, p1, k3; rep from *, end p2, k1.

Row 11 P1, k2, *p2, 1/1 RPC, p2, k2; rep from *, end p1.

Row 12 K1, p2, *k3, p1, k2, p2; rep from *, end k1.

Row 13 P1, k2, *p1, 1/1 RPC, p3; rep from *, end k2, p1.

Row 14 K1, p2, *k4, p1, k1, p2; rep from *, end k1.

Row 15 P1, k2, *1/1 RPC, p4, k2; rep from *, end p1.

Row 16 *P3, k5; rep from *, end p3, k1.

Row 17 P1, *k1, 1/1 RC, p5; rep from *, end k1, 1/1 RC.

Row 18 K1, p2, *k5, p3; rep from *, end k1.

Row 19 P1, *1/1 RC, k1, p5; rep from *, end 1/1 RC, p1.

Row 20 K1, p2, *k5, p3; rep from *, end k1.

Row 21 P1, *k2, 1/1 LPC, p4; rep from *, end k2, p1.

Row 22 Rep row 14.

Row 23 P1, *k2, p1, 1/1 LPC, p3; rep from *, end k2, p1.

Row 24 Rep row 12.

Row 25 P1, *k2, p2, 1/1 LPC, p2; rep from *, end k2, p1.

Row 26 Rep row 10.

Row 27 P1, *k2, p3, 1/1 LPC, p1; rep from *, end k2, p1.

Row 28 Rep row 8.

Row 29 P1, *k2, p4, 1/1 LPC; rep from *, end k2, p1.

Rows 30 to 34 Rep rows 2 to 6.

Row 35 *K3, p5; rep from *, end k3, p1.

Row 36 K1, p3, *k5, p3; rep from * to end.

Cont as desired.

circle fringe

▶ ▲ (multiple of 16 sts plus 5 after cords are joined)

Make desired number of Basic circles (an even number). *Insert dpn under 3 horizontal bars between sts at top of one circle. Join yarn and work St st cord (see page 188) for 2" (5cm), leave sts on needle (cut yarn). With same dpn, pick up 3 sts on next circle, join yarn and work St st cord for 1" (2.5cm), leave sts on needle and cut yarn. Rep from *.

Join cords

Row 1 (RS) *Single cast on 5 sts onto another needle, then with same needle, k3 cord sts; rep from *, end single cast on 5 sts.

Row 2 *K5, p3; rep from *, end k5.

Row 3 *P5, k3; rep from *, end p5.

Rep rows 2 and 3 until desired length.

Cont as desired.

circles

▶ ▲ (multiple of 10 sts plus 1 after circles are joined)

Basic circle

Invisibly cast on 5 sts. Work St st cord (see page 188) for 4" (10cm). Graft open sts to cast-on sts using Kitchener st (see page 188) to form a circle.

Make desired number of circles. Insert needle under 3 horizontal bars between sts at top of each circle.

Join circles

Row 1 (RS) Single cast on 4 sts onto another needle, *k3 sts from circle, single cast on 7 sts; rep from *, end last rep single cast on 4 sts.

Cont as desired.

closed circles

▼ ▶ ▲ Work same as for Circles, picking up sts at bottom and top of each circle.

stacked circles

▶ ▲ (multiple of 8 sts plus 5 after circles are joined)
Make desired number of Basic circles (see page 84).
Insert needle under 3 horizontal bars between sts at top of each circle.

Join first row of circles

Row 1 (RS) *Single cast on 5 sts onto another needle, then with same needle, k3 cord sts; rep from *, end single cast on 5 sts.

Cont in as desired.

Attach circles to each other at sides. Attach 2nd layer of circles to bottom of first layer (see photo).

square knots

▲ With MC, cast on desired number of sts. K 4 rows.
[With CC, k 2 rows, with MC, k 6 rows] twice.
Cont as desired.

Knots

(Work knots evenly spaced across edging.)
With RS facing, dpn, and CC, pick up and k1 st in 3 lower purl bumps and 2 upper purl bumps of first CC stripe—5 sts. Work St st cord (see page 188) for 3" (7.5cm), then k2tog, k1, k2tog, turn and p3tog. Fasten off last st.
Work another 5-st cord in purl bumps of 2nd CC stripe, directly above first cord. Rep for desired number of cords. Tie upper and lower cords tog to make square knots.

knotty knots

▲ **Main Pat**

(multiple of 10 sts)
Row 1 (RS) Knit.
Row 2 *K5, p5; rep from * to end.
Rep rows 1 and 2 until desired length.
Cont as desired.
Make one 3-st St st cord (see page 188) 3½" (9cm) long for each knot. Tie once and then sew cast-on and bound-off edges tog.
Attach knots along lower edge of main piece, centered under each St st panel. Knots can also be attached along center front edge of a cardigan and used as buttons.

stacked basketweave cord

▶ ▲ Work 3 separate lengths of Basketweave cord (see page 53). Sew one cord along edge of finished piece, then stack rem cords above first, alternating purl rows of Basketweave pat, as shown.

knit cord fringe

▶ ▲ Work as for knit cord loop. Cut loops and trim evenly.

knit cord loop

▶ ▲ Cast on 10 sts.
Row 1 (RS) Knit.
Row 2 (WS) Wyif sl 5 cord sts purlwise, bring yarn to back and k5.
Rep rows 1 and 2 for desired length, end with row 1.
Next row (WS) Bind off 4 sts, cut yarn and tie off st rem on RH needle, sl rem sts off needle and unravel them down to first row.
Knit cord loops.

appliqués

straight cord

Make any size cord (see pages 58-63) in length required for background piece. Fasten off. Sew cord to edge, placing as desired. See page 11 for how to sew cord to background

diagonals

Make any size cord (see pages 58-63), in length to fit on background piece. Fasten off. Sew ends diagonally in place. Follow photo for cord placement. Cont in this manner until desired number of cords are made. See page 11 for how to sew cord to background.

Note

• Unless noted, instructions or directional symbols are not given. Appliqués can be applied to any desired background.

xo's

Circle

Make any size cord (see pages 58–63), allowing at least 5"/12.5cm for each circle. Fasten off. Join ends of cord and form into a circle.

X's

Make 2 cords same size as cord for circle, allowing at least 2"/5cm for each cross.

Following photo for placement, sew circle and cross to background. See page 11 for how to sew cord to background.

cord scribble

Make any size cord (see pages 58–63), allowing at least 4"/10cm for each loop. Following photo to form scribble, sew cord in position on background. Fasten off when desired length. See page 11 for how to sew cord to background.

cross your hearts

Make any size St st cord (see page 188), allowing at least 9"/22.5cm for each heart. Following photo to form hearts, sew cord in position on background. Fasten off when desired length. See page 7 for how to sew cord to background.

basket o' flowers

(multiple of 10 sts plus 5)

Basket weave pattern

Rows 1, 3 and 5 (RS) K5, *p5, k5; rep from * to end.

Rows 2 and 4 Purl.

Rows 6, 8 and 10 K5, *p5, k5; rep from * to end.

Rows 7 and 9 Knit.

Rep rows 1 to 10 until desired length.

Cont as desired.

Flowers

Place slip knot on LH needle, *cast on 5 sts, bind off 5 sts, sl rem st back on LH needle, do not turn; rep from * 6 times more. Fasten off. Run threaded tapestry needle through straight edge of piece, pull tightly and secure. Cont in this manner until desired number of flowers are made. Sew flowers as desired to background. Embroider French knot in center of each flower.

box frames

(multiple of 16 sts plus 15)

• Each frame is worked separately, then all frames are joined on the same row.

Break yarn on all but last frame and leave sts on needle. Cast on 15 sts.

Rows 1 to 3 *K1, p1; rep from * to last st, k1.

Rows 4, 6, 8, 10, 12, 14 and 16 (RS) K1, p1, k11, p1, k1.

Rows 5, 7, 9, 11, 13, 15 and 17 K1, p1, k1, p9, k1, p1, k1.

Break yarn and leave sts on needle. On same needle, cast on and work as above to make another frame. Cont in this manner until desired number of frames are made.

To join frames, *[K1, p1] 7 times, k1, turn, cast on 1 st, turn; rep from * across to last frame, *[K1, p1] 7 times, k1.

Work 2 rows in seed st across all sts.

Cont as desired.

cord flower

Make any cord 15"/38cm. Bind off. Fold accordian syle until 6 petals are formed. Run thread through inner points of petal, pull tightly and secure. (See photo.)

Cont in this manner until desired number of flowers are made. Sew flowers as desired to background. Embellish as desired.

royal cord

Make any size cord (see pages 58–63), allowing at least 13"/33cm for each royal cord. Fasten off. Following photo to shape cord, sew cord in position on background. See page 11 for how to sew cord to background.

lazy daisy/basketweave background

Classic Basketweave

(multiple of 10 sts plus 5)

Rows 1, 3 and 5 (RS) K5, *p5, k5; rep from * to end.

Rows 2 and 4 P5, *k5, p5; rep from * to end.

Rows 6, 8 and 10 K5, *p5, k5; rep from * to end.

Rows 7 and 9 Rep row 2.

Rep rows 1 to 10 until desired length. Cont as desired.

Flowers

Place slip knot on LH needle, *cast on 10 sts, bind off 10 sts, sl RH needle through first cast on st, k and pass rem st on needle over it. Sl rem st back on LH needle, do not turn; rep from * 6 times more. Fasten off. Run threaded tapestry needle through straight edge of piece, pull tightly and secure. Cont in this manner until desired number of flowers are made. Sew flowers as desired to background. Embellish as desired.

leaves

• Each leaf is worked separately, then sewn onto background.

Cast on 5 sts.

Row 1 (RS) K2, yo, k1, yo, k2—7 sts.

Row 2 and all even rows Purl.

Row 3 K3, yo, k1, yo, k3—9 sts.

Row 5 K4, yo, k1, yo, k4—11 sts.

Row 7 Ssk, k7, k 2 tog—9 sts.

Row 9 Ssk, k5, k 2 tog—7 sts.

Row 11 Ssk, k3, k 2 tog—5 sts.

Row 13 Ssk, k1, k 2 tog—3 sts.

Row 15 SK2P—1 st. Fasten off.

Cont in this manner until desired number of leaves are made. Sew leaves to background following photo.

holly 'n berries

• Each leaf and berry are worked separately, then sewn onto background.

Holly

Cast on 5 sts.

Work 2 rows in St st.

Row 1 (RS) *Inc 1, k1, yo, k1, yo, k1, inc 1—9 sts.

Rows 2, 4, 6, 10, 12, 16 and 18 Purl.

Rows 3 and 9 K4, yo, k1, yo, k4—11 sts.

Rows 5 and 11 K5, yo, k1, yo, k5—13 sts.

Row 7 Bind off 3 sts, k2, yo, k1, yo, k6—12 sts.

Row 8 Bind off 3 sts, p8—9 sts.

Row 13 Bind off 3 sts, k9—10 sts.

Row 14 Bind off 3 sts, p6—7 sts.

Row 15 SKP, k3, k2tog—5 sts.

Row 17 SKP, k1, k2tog—3 sts.

Row 19 SK2P, fasten off.

Sew holly to desired background following photo.

Berries (make 3 for each holly)

Cast on 1 st. K in front, back, front, back and front again of st (5 sts made in one st).

Turn.

Rows 1 and 3 Knit.

Row 2 Purl.

Row 4 P2tog, p1, p2tog—3 sts.

Row 5 Knit.

Row 6 P3tog, fasten off.

Sew berries to background following photo.

le fleur

Cast on 35 sts.

Row 1 (WS) *K1, bind off 5 (2 sts on RH needle); rep from * to end—10 sts.

Run threaded tapestry needle through rem sts on needle, pull tightly and secure. Cont in this manner until desired number of flowers are made. Sew flowers to background as desired.

floral garland

(beg with multiple of 13 sts, end with multiple of 9 sts)

Row 1 (WS) *K1, bind off 11 (2 sts on needle); rep from * to end.

Row 2 K1, *turn, cast on 7 sts, turn, k2; rep from *, end last rep k1.

Row 3 Knit.

Cont as desired.

Make Le Fleur (above) and sew to each scallop as shown. Sew beads as desired.

passion flower

Cast on 4 sts

Row 1 (WS) K1, yo, k1, yo, k2—6 sts.

Rows 2 and 4 Knit.

Row 3 K2, yo, k2tog, yo, k2—7 sts.

Row 5 K3, yo, k2tog, yo, k2—8 sts.

Row 6 Bind off 4 sts, k to end—4 sts.

Repeat rows 1 to 6 six times more.

Run threaded tapestry needle through straight edge of piece, pull tightly and secure. Sew seam. Cont in this manner until desired number of flowers are made. Sew flowers as desired to background.

Make bobbles (see page 188). Sew beads and bobbles to flower as desired.

starburst

Cast on 6 sts

Rows 1 to 3 Knit.

Row 4 Sl1, k3, with LH needle lift 2nd, 3rd and 4th sts over first st, k2—3 sts.

Row 5 Knit.

Row 6 Cast on 3 sts, k to end—6 sts.

Repeat rows 1 to 6 four times more. Bind off.

Run threaded tapesty needle through straight edge of piece, pulling tightly and secure. Sew final bind off edge to cast on edge. Cont in this manner until desired number of starbursts are made. Sew starburst as desired.

t twist garter st flower

Cast on 40 sts.

Work 10 rows in garter st.

Row 11 (RS) *K5, rotate the LH needle counter-clockwise 360 degrees; rep from * to end.

Row 12 *P2tog; rep from * to end—20 sts.

Row 13 *K2tog; rep from * to end—10 sts.

Row 14 *P2tog; rep from * to end—5 sts.

Pass 2nd, 3rd, 4th and 5th st over first st. Fasten off.

Fold ends together and sew seam. Cont in this manner until desired number of flowers are made. Sew flowers as desired to background.

cabbage rose

Rose

Cast on 10 sts.

Row 1 (RS) Knit.

Row 2 and all even rows Purl.

Row 3 *K into front and back of st; rep from * to end—20 sts.

Row 5 *K into front and back of st; rep from * to end—40 sts.

Row 7 *K into front and back of st; rep from * to end—60 sts.

Row 9 *K into front and back of st; rep from * to end—80 sts.

Bind off.

Leaves

Cont in this manner until desired number of roses are made.

Sew roses and leaves as desired to background.

small disc (reversible)

- Each disc is worked separately, then sewn onto edge.
- Discs can be applied to edge evenly or alternating in placement as shown.

Cast on 15 sts loosely.

Work 2 rows in garter st.

Pass all sts, one at a time, over first st and fasten off. Cont in this manner until desired number of discs are made.

Sew disc to any edge as desired.

large disc (reversible)

- Each disc is worked separately, then sewn onto edge.
- Discs can be applied to edge evenly or alternating in placement.

Cast on 21 sts loosely.

Work 2 rows in garter st.

Pass all sts, one at a time, over first st and fasten off. Sew seam.

Cont in this manner until desired number of discs are made.

Sew disc to any edge as desired.

doughnuts (reversible)

Each doughnut is worked separately, then sewn onto edge.

Cast on 25 sts loosely.

Work 3 rows in garter st.

Pass all sts, one at a time, over 1st st and fasten off.

Cont in this manner until desired number of doughnuts are made.

Sew doughnut to any edge as desired.

floral diamond daisies

(multiple of 12 sts plus 14)

Daisies are embroidered after edge is knit .

2/1 RC Sl 1 st to cn and hold to back, k2, k1 from cn.

2/1 LC Sl 2 sts to cn and hold to front, k1, k2 from cn.

2/2 RC Sl 2 sts to cn and hold to back, k2, k2 from cn.

Knit 2 rows in garter st.

Row 1 (RS) K4, 2/1 RC, 2/1 LC, *k6, 2/1 RC, 2/1 LC; rep from * to last 4 sts, k4.

Row 2 and all even rows Purl.

Row 3 K3, 2/1 RC, k2, 2/1 LC, *k4, 2/1 RC, k2, 2/1 LC; rep from * to last 3 sts, k3.

Row 5 *K2, 2/1 RC, k4, 2/1 LC; rep from * to last 2 sts, k2.

Row 7 K1, *2/1 RC, k6, 2/1 LC; rep from * to last st, k1.

Row 9 K11, *2/2 RC, k8; rep from * to last 3 sts, k3.

Row 11 K1, *2/1 LC, k6, 2/1RC; rep from * to last st, k1.

Row 13 K2, *2/1 LC, k4, 2/1 RC, k2; rep from * to last 2 sts, k2.

Row 15 K3, 2/1 LC, k2, 2/1 RC, *k4, 2/1 LC, k2, 2/1 RC; rep from * to last 3 sts, k3.

Row 17 K4, 2/1 LC , 2/1 RC, *k6, 2/1 LC, 2/1 RC; rep from * to last 4 sts, k4.

Row 19 K5, 2/2 RC, *k8, 2/2 RC; rep from * to last 5 sts, k5.

Row 20 Purl.

Cont as desired.

colors

argyle

(multiple of 16 sts)

Colors Gray (A) and Blue (B)

Cast on with A. Work 6 rows in k2, p2 rib.

Work 4 rows in St st.

Work 15 rows of Argyle Chart.

Cont as desired.

Color Key

⬛ Gray (A)

⬜ Blue (B)

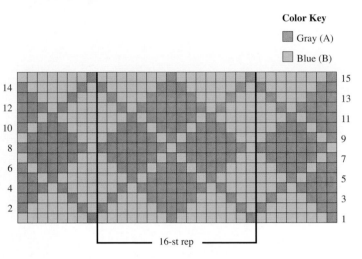

16-st rep

gingham

(multiple of 4 sts plus 2)

Colors Dark Blue (A), Light Blue (B) and White (C)

Note Sl sts purlwise with yarn at WS of work.

Cast on with A. Work 6 rows in k2, p2 rib.

Work 4 rows in St st.

Beg Gingham Pat

Row 1 (RS) With B, k1, sl 1, *k2, sl 2; rep from *, end k2, sl 1, k1.

Row 2 With B, p1, sl 1, *p2, sl 2; rep from *, end p2, sl 1, p1.

Row 3 With A, knit.

Row 4 With C, p2, *sl 2, p2; rep from * to end.

Row 5 With C, k2, *sl 2, k2; rep from * to end.

Row 6 With A, purl.

Rep rows 1 to 6 three times more.

Cont as desired.

petite print

(multiple of 4 sts plus 1)

Colors Gray (A) and Lavender (B)

Note Sl sts purlwise with yarn at WS of work.

Cast on with A. Work 6 rows in k2, p2 rib.

Work 4 rows in St st.

Beg Petite Print Pat

Row 1 (RS) With B, k1, sl 1, *k1, sl 3; rep from *, end k1, sl 1, k1.

Row 2 With B, k1, *p3, sl 1; rep from *, end p3, k1.

Row 3 With A, k2, *sl 1, k3; rep from *, end sl 1, k2.

Row 4 With A, k1, p to last st, k1.

Row 5 With B, k1, *sl 3, k1; rep from * to end.

Row 6 With B, k1, p1, *sl 1, p3; rep from *, end sl 1, p1, k1.

Row 7 With A, k4, *sl 1, k3; rep from * to last st, end k1.

Row 8 Rep row 4.

Rep rows 1 to 8 twice more.

Cont as desired.

houndstooth

(multiple of 4 sts)

Colors Gray (A), Pink (B), Green (C) and Blue (D)

Cast on with A. Work 4 rows in k2, p2 rib.

Work 12 rows of Houndstooth Chart once.

Cont as desired.

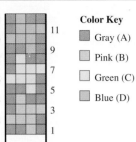

Color Key
- ■ Gray (A)
- □ Pink (B)
- □ Green (C)
- ■ Blue (D)

4-st rep

tweedy

(odd number of sts)

Colors Green (A) and Gray (B)

Note Sl sts purlwise with yarn at WS of work.

Cast on with A. K 2 rows.

Beg Tweedy Pat

Row 1 (RS) With B, k1, *sl 1, k1; rep from * to end.

Row 2 With B, purl.

Rows 3 and 4 With A, rep rows 1 and 2.

Row 5 With B, k2, *sl 1, k1; rep from * to last st, end k1.

Row 6 With B, purl.

Rows 7 and 8 With A, rep rows 5 and 6.

Rep rows 1 to 8 three times more.

Cont as desired.

garter stripe

Colors Green (A) and White (B)

Cast on with A.

K 4 rows A, [2 rows B, 2 rows A] 3 times, 2 rows B.

Cont as desired.

triangles

(multiple of 6 sts plus 3)

Colors Green (A) and Gray (B)

Note Sl sts purlwise with yarn at WS of work.

Cast on with A. K 2 rows.

Beg Triangles Pat

Row 1 (RS) With B, k1, *sl 1, k5; rep from *, end sl 1, k1.

Row 2 With B, k1, *sl 1, p5; rep from *, end sl 1, k1.

Row 3 With A, k3, *sl 3, k3; rep from * to end.

Row 4 With A, k1, p2, *sl 3, p3; rep from *, end sl 3, p2, k1.

Row 5 With B, k1, sl 2, *k3, sl 3; rep from *, end k3, sl 2, k1.

Row 6 With B, k1, sl 2, *p3, sl 3; rep from *, end p3, sl 2, k1.

Row 7 With A, k4, *sl 1, k5; rep from *, end sl 1, k4.

Row 8 With A, k1, p3, *sl 1, p5; rep from *, end sl 1, p3, k1.

Rep rows 1 to 8 three times more.

Cont as desired.

2-color slip st

(multiple of 6 sts plus 5)

Colors Blue (A) and White (B)

Note Sl sts purlwise with yarn in front (wyif) or with yarn in back (wyib).

Cast on with A. Work 5 rows in St st. K 1 row on WS for turning ridge.

Beg 2-Color Slip St Pat

Row 1 (RS) With B, knit.

Row 2 With B, purl.

Row 3 With A, k1, sl 3 wyib, *sl 3 wyif, sl 3 wyib; rep from *, end k1.

Row 4 With A, p1, sl 3 wyif, *sl 3 wyib, sl 3 wyif; rep from *, end p1.

Rows 5 and 6 Rep rows 1 and 2.

Row 7 With A, k1, sl 3 wyif, *sl 3 wyib, sl 3 wyif; rep from *, end k1.

Row 8 With A, p1, sl 3 wyib, *sl 3 wyif, sl 3 wyib; rep from *, end p1.

Rep rows 1 to 8 twice more.

Cont as desired.

Fold hem to WS at turning ridge and sew in place.

sugar twists

(multiple of 8 sts plus 5)

Colors White (A) and Blue (B)

Note Sl sts purlwise with yarn at WS of work.

1/2 RC Sl 2 sts to cn and hold to back, k1, k2 from cn.

Cast on with A. K 2 rows.

Beg Sugar Twists Pat

Row 1 (RS) With A, k5, *1/2 RC, k5; rep from * to end.

Row 2 With A, purl.

Rows 3 and 4 With B, [k1, sl 1] twice, k1, *sl 3, [k1, sl 1] twice, k1; rep from * to end.

Rep rows 1 to 4 six times more.

Cont as desired.

spiral ridge

(multiple of 3 sts)

Colors Black (A) and Blue (B)

Note Sl sts purlwise with yarn at WS of work.

1/1 RT Skip 1 st and k 2nd st, then k the skipped st; sl both sts off needle.

Cast on with A.

Preparation row (RS) With B, *k2, sl 1; rep from *, end k3.

Row 1 (WS) With B, p3, *sl 1, p2; rep from * to end.

Row 2 With A, k1, *1/1 RT, sl 1; rep from *, end k2.

Row 3 With A, *p2, sl 1; rep from *, end p3.

Row 4 With B, k1, *sl 1, 1/1 RT; rep from *, end sl 1, k1.

Row 5 With B, p1, *sl 1, p2; rep from *, end sl 1, p1.

Row 6 With A, *1/1 RT, sl 1; rep from *, end 1/1 RT, k1.

Row 7 With A, rep row 1.

Rows 8 and 9 With B, rep rows 2 and 3.

Rows 10 and 11 With A, rep rows 4 and 5.

Row 12 With B, rep row 6.

Rep rows 1 to 12 once more, then work row 1 once more.

Cont as desired.

3-color garter slip stripe

(odd number of sts)

Colors Dark Gray (A), Blue (B) and Light Gray (C)

Note Sl sts purlwise with yarn at WS of work.

Cast on with A. Work 5 rows in St st. K 1 row on WS for turning ridge.

Beg 3-Color Garter Slip Stripe Pat

Rows 1 and 2 With A, knit.

Rows 3 and 4 With B, *k1, sl 1; rep from *, end k1.

Rows 5 and 6 With C, knit.

Rows 7 and 8 With A, k2, *sl 1, k1; rep from *, end sl 1, k2.

Rows 9 and 10 With B, knit.

Rows 11 and 12 With C, rep rows 3 and 4.

Rows 13 and 14 With A, knit.

Rows 15 and 16 With B, rep rows 7 and 8.

Rows 17 and 18 With C, knit.

Rows 19 and 20 With A, rep rows 3 and 4.

Cont as desired.

Fold hem to WS at turning ridge and sew in place.

knotty stripes

(odd number of sts)

Colors Gray (A), Blue (B) and White (C)

Note Sl sts purlwise with yarn in back.

Cast on with A. Work 5 rows in St st. K 1 row on WS for turning ridge.

Beg Knotty Stripes Pat

Row 1 (RS) With A, knit.

Row 2 With A, k1, p to last st, k1.

Row 3 With B, k1, [k1, yo, k1] into next st, *sl 1, [k1, yo, k1] into next st; rep from *, end k1.

Row 4 With B, k1, k3tog tbl, *sl 1, k3tog tbl; rep from *, end k1.

Row 5 With A, knit.

Row 6 With A, k1, p to last st, k1.

Row 7 With C, k2, [k1, yo, k1] into next st, *sl 1, [k1, yo, k1] into next st; rep from *, end k2.

Row 8 With C, k1, p1, k3tog tbl, *sl 1, k3tog tbl; rep from *, end p1, k1.

Rep rows 1 to 8 once more.

Cont as desired.

Fold hem to WS at turning ridge and sew in place.

2-color garter slip stripe

(odd number of sts)

Colors Black (A) and Blue (B)

Note Sl sts purlwise with yarn at WS of work.

Cast on with A. Work 5 rows in St st. K 1 row on WS for turning ridge.

Beg 2-Color Garter Slip Stripe Pat

Rows 1 and 2 With B, knit.

Rows 3 and 4 With A, *k1, sl 1; rep from *, end k1.

Rows 5 and 6 With B, knit.

Rows 7 and 8 With A, k2, *sl 1, k1; rep from *, end sl 1, k2.

Rep rows 1 to 8 twice more, then work rows 1 and 2 once more.

Cont as desired.

Fold hem to WS at turning ridge and sew in place.

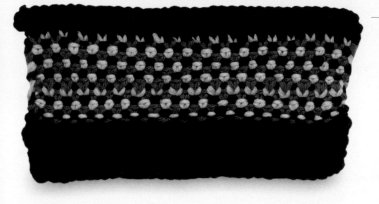

swiss dots

(odd number of sts)

Colors Pink (A) and Gray (B)

Note Sl sts purlwise with yarn at WS of work.

Cast on with A. Work 5 rows in St st. K 1 row on WS for turning ridge. K 1 row.

Beg Swiss Dots Pat

Row 1 (WS) With A, p1, *k1, p1; rep from * to end.

Row 2 With B, k1, *sl 1, k1; rep from * to end.

Row 3 With B, k1, *p1, k1; rep from * to end.

Row 4 With A, k2, sl 1, *k1, sl 1; rep from * to last 2 sts, k2.

Rep rows 1 to 4 seven times more, then work row 1 once more.

Cont as desired.

Fold hem to WS at turning ridge and sew in place.

tricolor linen st

(even number of sts)

Colors Black (A), Pink (B) and White (C)

Note: Sl sts purlwise with yarn in back (wyib) or with yarn in front (wyif), as directed.

Cast on with A.

Work 6 rows in k2, p2 rib.

K 1 row, p 1 row.

Beg Tricolor Linen St

Row 1 (RS) With B, k2, *wyif, sl 1, wyib, k1; rep from * to end.

Row 2 With C, p2, *wyib, sl 1, wyif, p1; rep from * to end.

Row 3 With A, rep row 1.

Row 4 With B, rep row 2.

Row 5 With C, rep row 1.

Row 6 With A, rep row 2.

Rep rows 1 to 6 twice more.

Cont as desired.

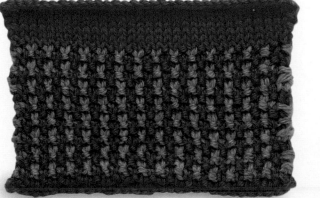

dots-dashes

(multiple of 10 sts plus 7)

Colors Gray (A) and Pink (B)

Note Sl sts purlwise with yarn at WS of work.

Cast on with A. Work 5 rows in St st. K 1 row on WS for turning ridge.

Beg Dots-Dashes Pat

Row 1 (RS) With B, knit.

Row 2 With B, purl.

Rows 3 and 4 With A, k1, *k5, sl 2, k1, sl 2; rep from *, end k6.

Rows 5 and 6 Rep rows 1 and 2.

Rows 7 and 8 With A, k1, *sl 2, k1, sl 2, k5; rep from * to last 6 sts, [sl 2, k1] twice.

Rep rows 1 to 8 once more, then work rows 1 and 2 once more.

Cont as desired.

Fold hem to WS at turning ridge and sew in place.

tweed blocks

(multiple of 10 sts plus 9)

Colors Gray (A) and Pink (B)

Note Sl sts purlwise with yarn at WS of work.

Cast on with A. Work 5 rows in St st. K 1 row on WS for turning ridge. Work 4 rows in St st.

Beg Tweed Blocks Pat

Row 1 (RS) With B, k1, sl 1, k1, *sl 3, [k1, sl 1] 3 times, k1; rep from * to last 6 sts, sl 3, k1, sl 1, k1.

Row 2 Rep row 1.

Row 3 With A, knit.

Row 4 With A, purl.

Rep rows 1 to 4 twice more, then work rows 1 and 2 once more.

Cont as desired.

Fold hem to WS at turning ridge and sew in place.

block weave

(multiple of 9 sts plus 6)

Colors Gray (A) and Pink (B)

Note Sl sts purlwise with yarn in front (wyif) or with yarn in back (wyib).

Cast on with A. Work 5 rows in St st. K 1 row on WS for turning ridge.

Beg Block Weave Pat

Row 1 (RS) With A, knit.

Row 2 With A, k2, p to last 2 sts, k2.

Row 3 With B, k2, *sl 2 wyib, k1, [sl 1 wyif, k1] 3 times; rep from *, end sl 2 wyib, k2.

Row 4 With B, k2, *sl 2 wyif, p7; rep from *, end sl 2 wyif, k2.

Row 5 With A, k4, *sl 1 wyif, [k1, sl 1 wyif] 3 times, k2; rep from * to last 2 sts, k2.

Row 6 With A, k2, p to last 2 sts, k2.

Rep rows 3 to 6 twice more.

Cont as desired.

Fold hem to WS at turning ridge and sew in place.

bricks

(multiple of 6 sts plus 3)

Colors Pink (A) and Gray (B)

Note Sl sts purlwise with yarn at WS of work.

Cast on with A. Work 5 rows in St st. K 1 row on WS for turning ridge.

Beg Bricks Pat

Row 1 (RS) With B, knit.

Row 2 With B, purl.

Rows 3, 4 and 6 With A, k4, sl 1, *k5, sl 1; rep from *, end k4.

Row 5 With A, p4, sl 1, *p5, sl 1; rep from *, end p4.

Row 7 With B, knit.

Row 8 With B, purl.

Rows 9, 10 and 12 With A, k1, sl 1, *k5, sl 1; rep from *, end k1.

Row 11 With A, p1, sl 1, *p5, sl 1; rep from *, end p1.

Rep rows 1 to 12 once more.

Cont as desired.

Fold hem to WS at turning ridge and sew in place.

mosaic print

(multiple of 8 sts plus 3)

Colors Lavender (A) and Gray (B)

Note Sl sts purlwise with yarn at WS of work.

Cast on with A. K 2 rows. With B, k 1 row, p 1 row.

Beg Mosaic Print Pat

Row 1 (RS) With A, k1, *sl 1, k7; rep from *, end sl 1, k1.

Row 2 Rep row 1.

Rows 3 and 4 With B, k4, *sl 1, k1, sl 1, k5; rep from * to last 7 sts, sl 1, k1, sl 1, k4.

Rows 5 and 6 With A, k3, *sl 1, k3; rep from * to end.

Rows 7 and 8 With B, k2, *sl 1, k5, sl 1, k1; rep from * to last st, k1.

Rows 9 and 10 With A, k5, *sl 1, k7; rep from * to last 6 sts, sl 1, k5.

Rows 11 and 12 Rep rows 7 and 8.

Rows 13 and 14 Rep rows 5 and 6.

Rows 15 and 16 Rep rows 3 and 4.

Rep rows 1 to 16 once more.

With A, k 2 rows.

Cont as desired.

pyramid

(multiple of 14 sts plus 3)

Colors Lavender (A) and Gray (B)

Note: Sl sts purlwise with yarn at WS of work.

Cast on with A. K 2 rows.

Beg Pyramid Pat

Row 1 (RS) With B, k8, *sl 1, k13; rep from *, end sl 1, k8.

Row 2 Rep row 1.

Rows 3 and 4 With A, k2, *[sl 1, k1] twice, sl 1, k3, [sl 1, k1] 3 times; rep from * to last st, k1.

Rows 5 and 6 With B, k7, *sl 1, k1, sl 1, k11; rep from * to last 10 sts, sl 1, k1, sl 1, k7.

Rows 7 and 8 With A, k2, *sl 1, k1, sl 1, k7, [sl 1, k1] twice; rep from * to last st, k1.

Rows 9 and 10 With B, k5, *[sl 1, k1] 3 times, sl 1, k7; rep from * to last 12 sts, [sl 1, k1] 3 times, sl 1, k5.

Rows 11 and 12 With A, k2, *sl 1, k11, sl 1, k1; rep from * to last st, k1.

Rows 13 and 14 With B, k3, *[sl 1, k1] 5 times, sl 1, k3; rep from * to end.

Rows 15 and 16 With A, k1, *sl 1, k13; rep from *, end sl 1, k1.

Rep rows 1 to 16 once more.

With A, k 2 rows.

Cont as desired.

diamond mosaic

(multiple of 10 sts plus 3)

Colors Lavender (A) and Gray (B)

Note Sl sts purlwise with yarn at WS of work.

Cast on with A. K 2 rows.

Beg Diamond Mosaic Pat

Row 1 (RS) With B, k1, *sl 1, k9; rep from *, end sl 1, k1.

Row 2 Rep row 1.

Row 3 With A, k3, *[sl 1, k1] 3 times, sl 1, k3; rep from * to end.

Row 4 With A, p3, *[sl 1, k1] 3 times, sl 1, p3; rep from * to end.

Rows 5 and 6 With B, k2, *sl 1, k7, sl 1, k1; rep from * to last st, k1.

Row 7 With A, *k4, [sl 1, k1] 3 times; rep from * to last 3 sts, k3.

Row 8 With A, p4, [sl 1, k1] twice, sl 1, *p5, [sl 1, k1] twice, sl 1; rep from *, end p4.

Rows 9 and 10 With B, [k1, sl 1] twice, *k5, [sl 1, k1] twice, sl 1; rep from * to last 9 sts, k5, [sl 1, k1] twice.

Row 11 With A, k5, sl 1, k1, sl 1, *k7, sl 1, k1, sl 1; rep from *, end k5.

Row 12 With A, p5, sl 1, k1, sl 1, *p7, sl 1, k1, sl 1; rep from *, end p5.

Rows 13 and 14 With B, k2, sl 1, k1, sl 1, k3, *[sl 1, k1] 3 times, sl 1, k3; rep from * to last 5 sts, sl 1, k1, sl 1, k2.

Row 15 With A, k6, *sl 1, k9; rep from *, end sl 1, k6.

Row 16 With A, p6, *sl 1, p9; rep from *, end sl 1, p6.

Rows 17 to 20 Rep rows 9 to 12.

Rows 21 to 24 Rep rows 5 to 8.

Rows 25 and 26 Rep rows 1 and 2.

With A, k 2 rows.

Cont as desired.

bubble wrap

(multiple of 5 sts plus 1)

Colors Gray (A) and White (B)

Note Sl sts purlwise with yarn at WS of work.

Cast on with A. Work 5 rows in St st. K 1 row on WS for turning ridge. Work 3 rows in St st.

Beg Bubble Wrap Pat

Row 1 (WS) With A, p1, *p1 wrapping yarn twice around needle (instead of once), p2, p1 wrapping yarn twice, p1; rep from * to end.

Row 2 With B, k1, sl 1 (dropping extra loop), k2, sl 1 (dropping extra loop), *[k1, yo, k1, yo, k1] into next st, sl 1 (dropping extra loop), k2, sl 1 (dropping extra loop); rep from *, end k1.

Row 3 With B, p1, sl 1, p2, sl 1, *k5, sl 1, p2, sl 1; rep from *, end p1.

Row 4 With B, k1, sl 1, k2, sl 1, *p5, sl 1, k2, sl 1; rep from *, end k1.

Row 5 With B, p1, sl 1, p2, sl 1, *k2tog, k3tog, pass k2tog st over k3tog st, sl 1, p2, sl 1; rep from *, end p1.

Row 6 With A, k1, *drop first elongated st off needle, sl 2, drop next elongated st off needle, then with LH needle, pick up first elongated st, sl 2 sts from RH needle back to LH needle, then pick up 2nd elongated st with LH needle, k5; rep from * to end.

Row 7 With A, purl.

Row 8 With A, knit.

Rep rows 1 to 6 once more.

Cont as desired.

Fold hem to WS at turning ridge and sew in place.

bobble chevron classic

(multiple of 12 sts plus 3)

Colors Gray (A), Lavender (B), Blue (C) and Pink (D)

Make Bobble (MB) K into front, back, front, back and front of same st—5 sts; turn, p5, turn, k5, turn, p5, pass 2nd, 3rd, 4th and 5th sts, one at a time, over first st. Tie off last st.

Cast on with A.

Beg Bobble Chevron Classic Pat

Row 1 (RS) K1, ssk, *k9, SK2P; rep from * to last 12 sts, k9, k2tog, k1.

Row 2 K1, *p1, k4, [k1, yo, k1] in next st, k4; rep from *, end p1, k1.

Rep rows 1 and 2 in the following color sequence: 2 rows each with B, A, C, A, D and A. Cont as desired.

Make bobbles, alternating colors, and sew to points at lower edge.

french checks

(multiple of 4 sts plus 3)

Colors Gray (A), Light Blue (B), Dark Blue (C) and Lavender (D)

Note Sl sts purlwise with yarn at WS of work.

Cast on with A. Work 5 rows in St st. K 1 row on WS for turning ridge.

Beg French Checks Pat

Row 1 (RS) With B, k1, *sl 1, k3; rep from *, end sl 1, k1.

Row 2 With B, p1, *sl 1, p3; rep from *, end sl 1, p1.

Row 3 With C, *k3, sl 1; rep from *, end k3.

Row 4 With C, *p3, sl 1; rep from *, end p3.

Rows 5 and 6 With D, rep rows 1 and 2.

Rows 7 and 8 With A, rep rows 3 and 4.

Rep rows 1 to 8 twice more.

Cont as desired.

Fold hem to WS at turning ridge and sew in place.

garter st patchwork

(multiple of 5 sts)

Colors Light Gray (A), Blue (B), Yellow (C), Lavender (D), Light Green (E) and Pink (F)

Notes 1 Work each 5-st, 8-row block in colors as desired. **2** Bring new yarn under old yarn at color change to prevent holes.

Cast on with A.

K 1 row on WS.

Beg Garter St Patchwork Pat

Row 1 (RS) With desired color, k5, *with next color, k5; rep from * to end.

Rows 2 to 8 Knit, matching colors of preceding rows.

Row 9 Rep row 1, changing colors of all blocks.

Rows 10 to 16 Knit, matching colors of preceding rows.

Cont as desired.

chevron tassel/bobble/fringe

(multiple of 14 sts plus 2)

Colors Gray (A) and Pink (B)

Make Bobble Work as for Bobble Chevron Classic.

Cast on with A

Beg Chevron Tassel Pat

Rows 1 and 3 (WS) Purl.

Rows 2 and 4 K1, k into front and back of next st, k4, ssk, k2tog, k4, *[k into front and back of next st] twice, k4, ssk, k2tog, k4; rep from * to last 2 sts, k into front and back of next st, k1.

Rows 5 to 8 With B, rep rows 1 to 4.

Cont as desired.

With B, make bobbles or fringe and attach to points of lower edge.

garter st puff stripe

(multiple of 8 sts plus 4)

Colors Gray (A) and Lavender (B)

Notes 1 Carry yarn across back of work, pulling a little on the yarn to make the garter st stripes puff out. **2** On WS rows, remember to bring old yarn to front of work before picking up new yarn.

Cast on with A.

Beg Garter St Puff Stripe Pat

Row 1 (RS) *K4A, k4B; rep from *, end k4A.

Rows 2 to 14 Rep row 1.

Cont as desired.

3-color garter stripe

(any number of sts)

Colors Blue (A), Pink (B) and Lavender (C)

Cast on with A.

Beg with a RS row, *k 2 rows each with A, B and C; rep from * once more, then k 2 rows with A.

Cont as desired.

shadowbox fringed

(multiple of 4 sts plus 3)

Colors White (A), Black (B) and Gray (C)

Note Sl sts purlwise with yarn at WS of work.
Cast on with A.

Beg Shadowbox Pat

Row 1 (RS) With A, knit.

Row 2 With A, k1, *k 1 wrapping yarn twice around needle, k3; rep from *, end k1 wrapping yarn twice around needle, k1.

Row 3 With B, k1, *sl 1 dropping extra wrap, k3; rep from *, end sl 1 dropping extra wrap, k1.

Row 4 With B, k1, *sl 1, k3; rep from *, end sl 1, k1.

Row 5 With C, k1, *sl 2, k2; rep from *, end sl 1, k1.

Row 6 With C, k1, sl 1, *p2, sl 2; rep from *, end k1.

Rep rows 1 to 6 twice more.

With A, k 2 rows.

Cont as desired.

With A, work fringe along lower edge, centering each fringe under A sl sts.

plaid

(multiple of 6 sts plus 1)

Colors Gray (A), Black (B) and Red (C)

Note If desired, work vertical stripes of chart using duplicate st after border is complete.

Cast on with A.

Work 6 rows in k2, p2 rib.

Work 6 rows of Plaid Chart twice, then work row 1 once more.

Cont as desired.

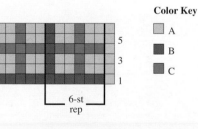

Color Key

- ☐ A
- ■ B
- ■ C

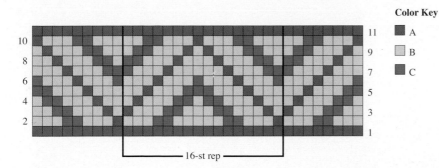

Color Key
- A
- B
- C

16-st rep

chic chevron

(multiple of 16 sts plus 1)

Colors Black (A), Gray (B) and Red (C)

Cast on with A.

K 1 row on WS.

Work 11 rows of Chic Chevron Chart.

Cont as desired.

au petite

(multiple of 6 sts plus 3)

Colors Black (A), Gray (B) and Red (C)

Cast on with A.

Work 9 rows of Au Petite Chart.

Cont as desired.

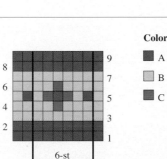

Color Key
- A
- B
- C

6-st rep

mock eyelet

(odd number of sts)

Colors Red (A), Gray (B) and Black (C)

Note Sl sts purlwise with yarn at WS of work.

Cast on with A.

Beg Mode Eyelet Pat

Row 1 (WS) Knit.

Row 2 Knit.

Row 3 Purl.

Rows 4 and 5 With B, knit.

Rows 6 and 7 With C, k1, *sl 1, k1; rep from * to end.

Rows 8 and 9 With B, knit.

Rows 10, 12, 13 and 14 With A, knit.

Row 11 With A, purl.

Row 15 With A, knit.

Cont as desired.

slip st vertical stripe

(multiple of 4 sts)

Colors Red (A) and White (B)

Note Sl sts purlwise with yarn at WS of work.

Cast on with A.

P 1 row on WS.

Beg Slip St Vertical Stripe Pat

Row 1 (RS) With B, k1, *sl 2, k2; rep from *, end sl 2, k1.

Row 2 With B, p1, *sl 2, p2; rep from *, end sl 2, p1.

Row 3 With A, k1, *k2, sl 2; rep from *, end k3.

Row 4 With A, p1, *p2, sl 2; rep from *, end p3.

Rep rows 1 to 4 until desired length.

Cont as desired.

cracked window

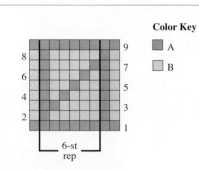

Color Key

■ A
□ B

(multiple of 6 sts plus 3)

Colors Black (A) and Gray (B)

Cast on with A.

P 1 row on WS.

Work 9 rows of Cracked Window Chart.

Cont as desired.

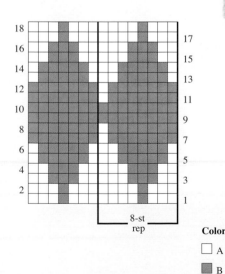

Color Key

□ A
■ B

diamonds

(multiple of 8 sts plus 7)

Colors White (A) and Black (B)

Cast on with A.

Work 6 rows in k2, p2 rib.

K 1 row, p 1 row.

Work 18 rows of Diamonds Chart.

Cont as desired.

florettes

(multiple of 6 sts plus 5)

Colors Pink (A) and Black (B)

Cast on with A.

Work 6 rows in k2, p2 rib.

K 1 row, p 1 row.

Work 6 rows of Florettes Chart twice.

Cont as desired.

Color Key
- A
- B

6-st
rep

alternating diamonds

(multiple of 8 sts plus 1)

Colors Black (A) and Yellow (B)

Cast on with A.

Work 6 rows in k2, p2 rib.

K 1 row, p 1 row.

Work 16 rows of Alternating Diamonds Chart.

Cont as desired.

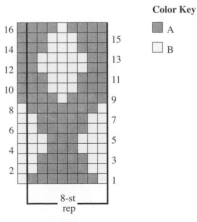

Color Key
- A
- B

8-st
rep

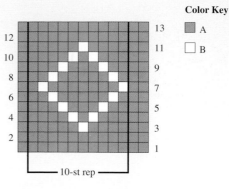

single diamonds

(multiple of 10 sts plus 3)

Colors Gray (A) and White (B)

Cast on with A. K 2 rows.

Work 13 rows of Single Diamonds Chart.

Cont as desired.

Color Key
- A
- B

10-st rep

double diamonds

(multiple of 14 sts plus 5)

Colors Gray (A) and White (B)

Cast on with A. K 2 rows.

Work 13 rows of Double

Diamonds Chart.

Cont as desired.

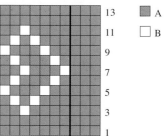

Color Key
- A
- B

14-st rep

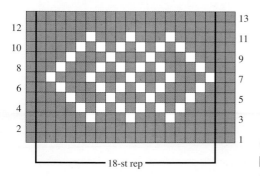

18-st rep

Color Key
- A
- B

triple diamonds

(multiple of 18 sts plus 3)

Colors Gray (A) and White (B)

Cast on with A. K 2 rows.

Work 13 rows of Triple Diamonds Chart.

Cont as desired.

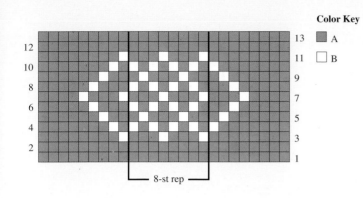

8-st rep

Color Key
■ A
□ B

diamond interlocks

(multiple of 8 sts plus 1)

Colors Gray (A) and White (B)

Cast on with A. K 2 rows.

Work 13 rows of Diamond Interlocks Chart.

Cont as desired.

6-st rep   6-st rep

Color Key
■ A
□ B

open or solid diamonds

(multiple of 6 sts plus 3)

Colors Gray (A) and White (B)

Cast on with A. K 2 rows.

Work 9 rows of Open or Solid Diamonds Chart.

Cont as desired.

diamond/bird's eye

(multiple of 6 sts plus 3)

Colors Gray (A), White (B) and Pink (C)

Cast on with A. K 2 rows.

Work 7 rows of Diamond/Bird's Eye Chart.

Cont as desired.

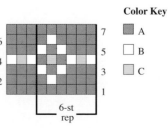

6-st rep

Color Key
■ A
□ B
□ C

petite diamonds

(multiple of 4 sts plus 1)

Colors Black (A), Gray (B) and Pink (C)

Cast on with A. K 2 rows.

Work 13 rows of Petite Diamonds Chart.

Cont as desired.

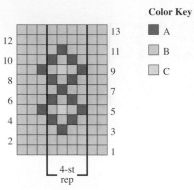

Color Key

◼ A
◼ B
◻ C

4-st rep

styles

(multiple of 12 sts plus 3)

Colors Black (A), Lavender (B) and White (C)

Cast on with A.

Work 18 rows of Styles Chart.

Cont as desired.

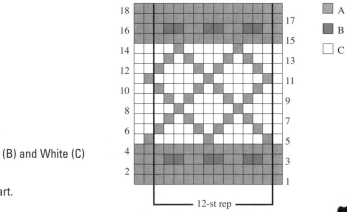

Color Key

◼ A
◼ B
◻ C

12-st rep

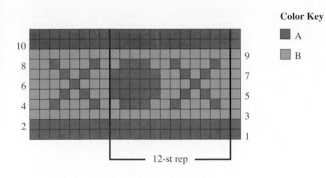

Color Key
- A
- B

x's and o's I

(multiple of 12 sts plus 9)

Colors Black (A) and Lavender (B)

Cast on with A. K 2 rows.

Work 11 rows of X's and O's I Chart.

Cont as desired.

12-st rep

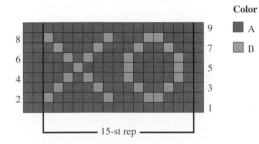

Color Key
- A
- B

x's and o's II

(multiple of 15 sts plus 3)

Colors Black (A) and Lavender (B)

Cast on with A. K 2 rows.

Work 9 rows of X's and O's II Chart.

Cont as desired.

15-st rep

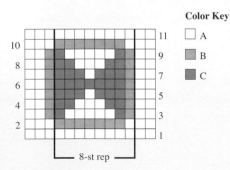

Color Key
- A
- B
- C

delta

(multiple of 8 sts plus 5)

Colors White (A), Black (B) and Lavender (C)

Cast on with A. K 2 rows.

Work 11 rows of Delta Chart.

Cont as desired.

8-st rep

op art I

(multiple of 4 sts plus 1)

Colors White (A), Black (B) and Pink (C)

Cast on with A. K 2 rows.

Work 9 rows of Op Art I Chart.

Cont as desired.

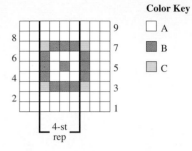

Color Key

☐ A
▨ B
☐ C

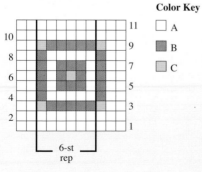

op art II

(multiple of 5 sts)

Colors White (A), Black (B) and Pink (C)

Cast on with A. K 2 rows.

Work 10 rows of Op Art II Chart.

Cont as desired.

Color Key

☐ A
▨ B
☐ C

Color Key

☐ A
▨ B
☐ C

op art III

(multiple of 6 sts plus 5)

Colors White (A), Black (B) and Pink (C)

Cast on with A. K 2 rows.

Work 11 rows of Op Art III Chart.

Cont as desired.

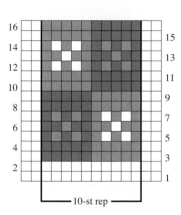

Color Key

☐ A
▨ B
▩ C

block block

(multiple of 10 sts plus 4)

Colors White (A), Black (B) and Magenta (C)

Cast on with A. K 2 rows.

Work 16 rows of Block Block Chart.

Cont as desired.

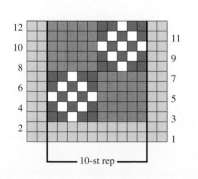

Color Key

▨ A
▨ B
▨ C
☐ D

diamond block

(multiple of 10 sts plus 4)

Colors Pink (A), Black (B), Magenta (C)
and White (D)

Cast on with A. K 2 rows.

Work 12 rows of Diamond Block Chart.

Cont as desired.

2-color plaited cable

(multiple of 4 sts)

Colors Black (A) and Beige (B)

2/2 RC Sl 2 A sts to cn and hold to back, k2B, k2A from cn.

2/2 LC Sl 2 A sts to cn and hold to front, k2B, k2A from cn.

Cast on with A.

P 1 row on WS.

Beg 2-color plaited cable

Row 1 (RS) *K2A, k2B; rep from * to end.

Row 2 and all WS rows Purl, matching colors of preceding row.

Rows 3 and 7 *2/2 RC; rep from * to end.

Rows 5 and 9 K2A, *2/2 LC; rep from * to last 2 sts, k2B.

Row 10 Rep row 2.

Cont as desired.

Color Key

- ▦ A
- ▪ B

```
6 |  |  |  |  |  |  |  |  |  |
                              5
4 |  |  |  |  |  |  |  |  |  |
                              3
2 |  |  |  |  |  |  |  |  |  |
                              1
  |_____|
    4-st
    rep
```

ric rac

(multiple of 4 sts plus 1)

Colors Beige (A) and Black (B)

Cast on with A.

Work 5 rows in St st, then k 1 row on WS for turning ridge.

Work 6 rows of Ric Rac Chart.

Work 4 rows in St st with A.

Work 6 rows of Ric Rac Chart.

Cont as desired.

Fold hem to WS at turning ridge and sew in place.

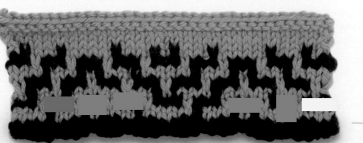

rippled chevron

(multiple of 16 sts plus 3)

Colors Black (A) and Beige (B)

Note Sl sts purlwise with yarn at WS of work.

Cast on with A.

Work 5 rows in St st, then k 1 row on WS for turning ridge.

K 1 row, p 1 row.

Beg Rippled Chevron Pat

Row 1 (RS) With B, k4, *sl 1, k3, sl 1, k1, sl 1, k3, sl 1, k5; rep from *, end last rep k4, instead of k5.

Row 2 P4, *sl 1, p3, sl 1, p1, sl 1, p3, sl 1, p5; rep from *, end last rep p4, instead of p5.

Row 3 With A, k3, *sl 1, k3; rep from * to end.

Row 4 P3, *sl 1, p3; rep from * to end.

Row 5 With B, k2, *sl 1, k3, sl 1, k5, sl 1, k3, sl 1, k1; rep from * to last st, k1.

Row 6 P2, *sl 1, p3, sl 1, p5, sl 1, p3, sl 1, p1; rep from * to last st, p1.

Row 7 With A, k1, *sl 1, k3; rep from *, end sl 1, k1.

Row 8 P1, *sl 1, p3; rep from *, end sl 1, p1.

Rep rows 1 to 6 once more.

Cont as desired.

small checks

(multiple of 4 sts)

Colors Beige (A) and Black (B)

Cast on with A.

K 4 rows.

Work 6 rows of Small Checks Chart once, then work rows 1 to 3 once more.

Cont as desired.

Color Key
■ A
■ B

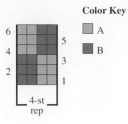

6
4
2
5
3
1

4-st rep

medium checks

(multiple of 6 sts)

Colors Black (A) and Beige (B)

Cast on with A.

K 4 rows.

Work 6 rows of Medium Checks Chart once, then work rows 1 to 3 once more.

Cont as desired.

Color Key
■ A
■ B

6
4
2
5
3
1

6-st rep

big checks

(multiple of 10 sts plus 5)

Colors Beige (A) and Black (B)

Cast on with A.

K 4 rows.

Work 10 rows of Big Checks Chart once.

Cont as desired.

Color Key
■ A
■ B

10
8
6
4
2
9
7
5
3
1

10-st rep

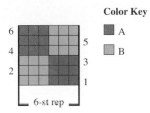

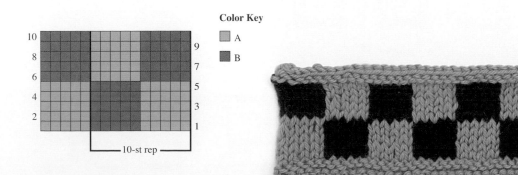

up and down I

(multiple of 12 sts plus 5)

Colors Green (A) and Black (B)

Cast on with A. K 2 rows.

Work 10 rows of Up and Down I Chart.

Cont as desired.

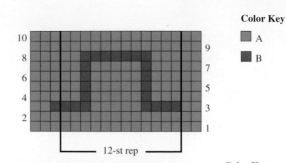

Color Key
- A
- B

up and down II

(multiple of 12 sts plus 5)

Colors Olive Green (A), Black (B) and Light Green (C)

Cast on with A. K 2 rows.

Work 9 rows of Up and Down II Chart.

Cont as desired.

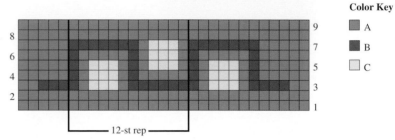

Color Key
- A
- B
- C

maze

(multiple of 8 sts plus 1)

Colors Light Green (A), Olive Green (B) and Black (C)

Cast on with A. K 2 rows.

Work 10 rows of Maze Chart.

Cont as desired.

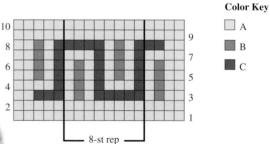

Color Key
- A
- B
- C

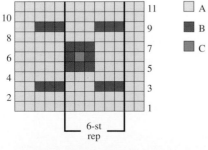

Color Key
- A
- B
- C

dot dash

(multiple of 6 sts plus 1)

Colors Light Green (A), Black (B) and Olive (C)

Cast on with A. K 2 rows.

Work 11 rows of Dot Dash Chart.

Cont as desired.

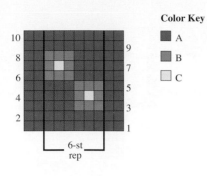

go go I

(multiple of 6 sts plus 4)

Colors Black (A), Olive Green (B) and Light Green (C)

Cast on with A. K 2 rows.

Work 10 rows of Go Go I Chart.

Cont as desired.

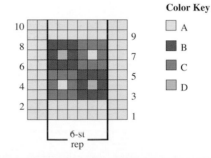

go go II

(multiple of 6 sts plus 4)

Colors Light Green (A), Black (B), Olive Green (C) and Gold (D)

Cast on with A. K 2 rows.

Work 10 rows of Go Go II Chart.

Cont as desired.

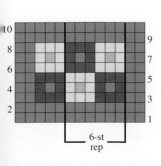

go go III

(multiple of 6 sts plus 1)

Colors Olive Green (A), Black (B), Light Green (C) and Gold (D)

Cast on with A. K 2 rows.

Work 10 rows of Go Go III Chart.

Cont as desired.

big apple

(multiple of 18 sts)

Colors Black (A), White (B), Dark Red (C), Light Red (D), Brown (E) and Olive Green (F)

Cast on with A. K 4 rows.

Work 22 rows of Big Apple Chart.

Cont as desired.

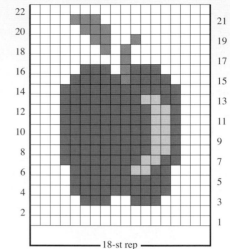

Color Key

☐ B
◼ C
◻ D
◼ E
◼ F

18-st rep

cherries

(multiple of 29 sts plus 2)

Colors Black (A), White (B), Red (C), Olive Green (D) and Brown (E)

Cast on with A. K 2 rows.

Work 24 rows of Cherries Chart.

Cont as desired.

Embroider Stem St.

Color Key

☐ B
◼ C
◻ D
◼ E

▮ Stem St with E

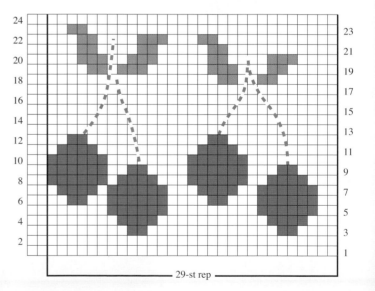

29-st rep

Color Key

☐ B
◼ C
◻ D

▮ Stem St with E

6-st rep

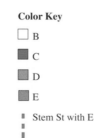

apple a day

(multiple of 6 sts plus 3)

Colors Black (A), White (B), Red (C), Olive Green (D) and Brown (E)

Cast on with A. K 2 rows.

Work 12 rows of Apple a Day Chart.

Cont as desired.

Embroider Stem St.

gingham check

(multiple of 10 sts plus 5)

Colors White (A) and Red (B)

Cast on with A.

Work 6 rows in k2, p2 rib.

K 1 row, p 1 row.

Work 12 rows of Gingham Check Chart. Work rows 1 to 5 once more.

Cont as desired.

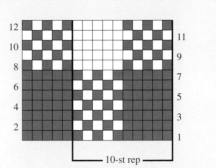

Color Key
☐ A
■ B

⊢ 10-st rep ⊣

slip st scallop with embroidery or fringe

(multiple of 8 sts plus 6)

Colors Red (A) and White (B)

Note Sl sts purlwise with yarn at WS of work.

Cast on with A.

Beg Sl St Scallop Pat

Row 1 (RS) With A, knit.

Row 2 Rep row 1.

Rows 3, 5 and 7 With B, k2, *sl 2, k6; rep from *, end sl 2, k2.

Rows 4, 6 and 8 With B, p2, *sl 2, p6; rep from *, end sl 2, p2.

Rows 9 to 12 With A, knit.

Cont as desired.

With A, embroider Star St in each B square or make fringe and attach to lower edge, centered beneath sl st columns.

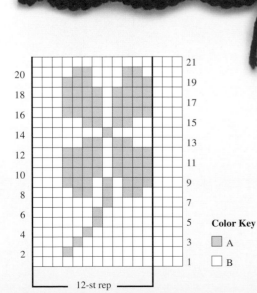

Cross Stitch   **Duplicate Stitch**   **Intarsia**

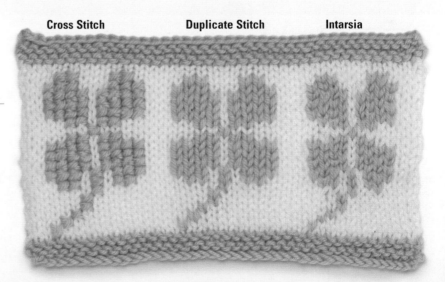

shamrock

(multiple of 12 sts plus 3)

Note Chart motif can be knit in, or embroidered after the piece is knit, using cross stitch or duplicate st (see page 189).

Colors Green (A) and White (B)

Cast on with A. K 4 rows.

Work 21 rows of Shamrock Chart.

Cont as desired.

Color Key
▨ A
☐ B

⊢ 12-st rep ⊣

bird's eye check

(odd number of sts)

Colors Red (A) and White (B)

Cast on with A.

K 5 rows.

Beg with a WS row, work 2 rows of Bird's Eye Check Chart 4 times, then work row 1 once more.

Cont as desired.

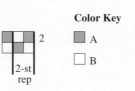

Color Key

A

B

2-st rep

slip st blocks

(multiple of 4 sts plus 3)

Colors White (A) and Red (B)

Note Sl sts purlwise with yarn at WS of work.

Cast on with A.

P 1 row on WS.

Beg Sl St Blocks Pat

Rows 1 and 3 (RS) With B, k3, *sl 1, k3; rep from * to end.

Rows 2 and 4 Rep row 1.

Rows 5 and 6 With A, knit.

Rep rows 1 to 6 twice more.

Cont as desired.

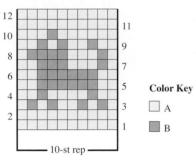

marching dogs

(multiple of 10 sts)

Colors Light Gray (A) and Black (B)

Cast on with A. K 2 rows.

Work 12 rows of Marching Dogs Chart.

Cont as desired.

Color Key
- ☐ A
- ▨ B

scottie dog

(multiple of 33 sts plus 2)

Colors Black (A) and Light Gray (B)

Cast on with A.

Work 29 rows of Scottie Dog Chart.

Cont as desired.

Color Key
- ▨ A
- ☐ B

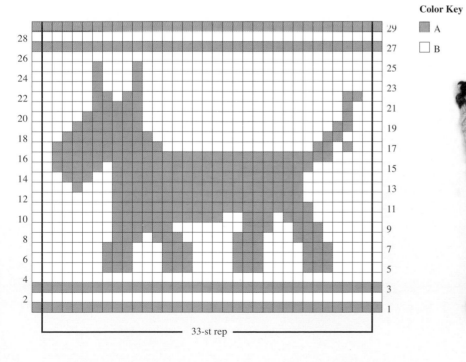

33-st rep

cat silhouette

(multiple of 19 sts)

Colors Blue (A), White (B), Black (C), Pink (D) and small amount of white mohair for whiskers (E)

Cast on with A. K 4 rows.

Work 23 rows of Cat Silhouette Chart.

Cont as desired.

Embroider Straight St.

■ A
□ B
■ C
■ D
⊟ Straight St with E

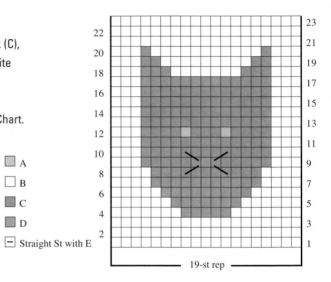

19-st rep

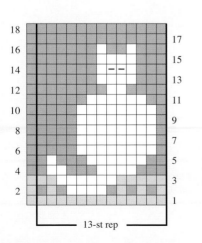

13-st rep

Color Key

■ A
■ B
□ C
⊟ Straight St with D

cat on a fence

(multiple of 13 sts plus 1)

Colors Dark Blue (A), Light Blue (B), White Angora (C) and Black (D)

Cast on with A. K 2 rows.

Work 18 rows of Cat on a Fence Chart.

Cont as desired.

Embroider Straight St.

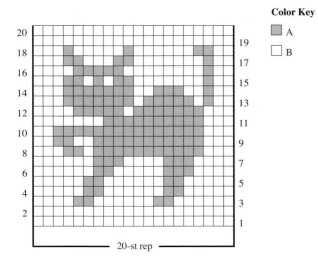

20-st rep

playful kitty

(multiple of 20 sts)

Colors Blue (A) and White (B)

Cast on with A. K 2 rows.

Work 20 rows of Playful Kitty Chart.

Cont as desired.

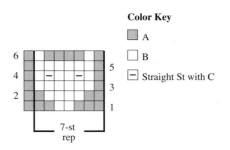

7-st rep

here kitty

(multiple of 7 sts plus 1)

Colors Blue (A), White (B) and Black (C)

Cast on with A. K 4 rows.

Work 6 rows of Here Kitty Chart.

Cont as desired.

Embroider Straight St.

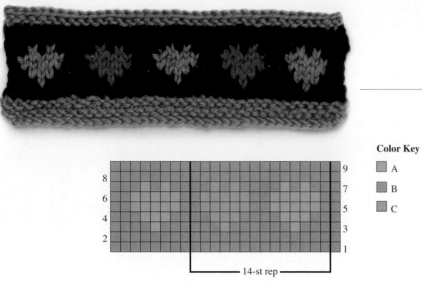

heart repeats

(multiple of 14 sts plus 9)

Colors Lavender (A), Black (B) and Pink (C)

Cast on with A. K 4 rows.

Work 9 rows of Heart Repeats Chart.

Cont as desired.

Color Key
- A
- B
- C

14-st rep

petite hearts

(multiple of 10 sts plus 3)

Colors Dark Pink (A), White (B) and Light Pink (C)

Cast on with A.

K 2 rows.

Work 18 rows of Petite Hearts Chart.

Cont as desired.

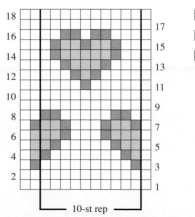

Color Key
- A
- B
- C

10-st rep

pierced hearts

(over 41 sts)

Colors Gray (A), White (B), Red (C) and Pink (D)

Cast on with A.

K 4 rows.

Work 14 rows of Pierced Hearts Chart.

Cont as desired.

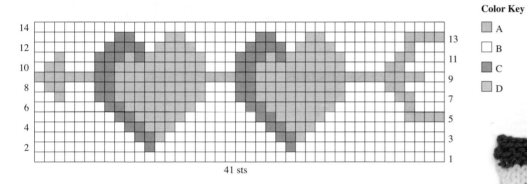

41 sts

Color Key

A
B
C
D

small hearts

(multiple of 10 sts plus 5)

Colors Pink (A), White (B), Yellow (C) and Blue (D)

Cast on with A.

K 4 rows.

Work 12 rows of Small Hearts Chart (alternating color of heart motif in each 10-st rep across row). Cont as desired.

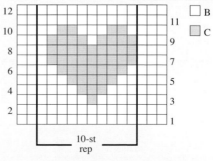

10-st rep

Color Key

B
C

bunny hop

(multiple of 18 sts plus 4)

Colors Light Green (A), Olive Green (B), Brown (C) and Blue (D)

Cast on with A.

Work 20 rows of Bunny Hop Chart.

Cont as desired.

Embroider French Knot.

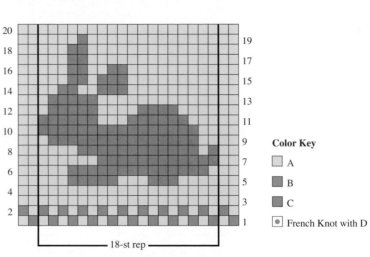

Color Key

- A
- B
- C
- ⊙ French Knot with D

18-st rep

baa baa

(multiple of 36 sts plus 1)

Colors Olive Green (A), Light Green (B), Black (C), White (D), and Blue (E)

Cast on with A.

Work 18 rows of Baa Baa Chart.

Cont as desired.

Embroider French Knots.

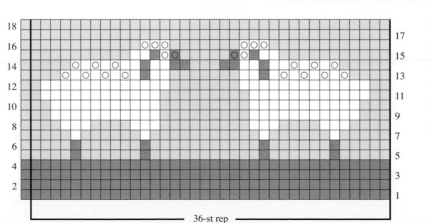

Color Key

- A
- B
- C
- D
- ○ French Knot with D
- ◉ French Knot with E

36-st rep

bold flower

(multiple of 45 sts plus 7)

Note If desired, embroider flowers and leaves using Straight St and Stem St, or sew on beads using matching sewing thread.

Colors Pink (A), White (B), Light Green (C), Olive Green (D) and Dark Pink (E)

Cast on with A. K 2 rows.

Work 18 rows of Bold Flower Chart.

Cont as desired.

Embroider Straight and Stem Sts or sew on beads.

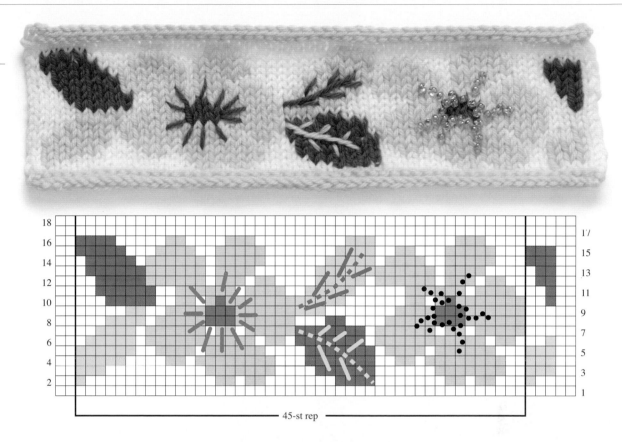

Color Key

- A
- B
- C
- D
- E
- Straight St with C
- Straight St with D
- Stem St with C
- Stem St with D
- Straight St with E
- ● Place Bead

45-st rep

blossom

(multiple of 16 sts plus 1)

Colors Pink (A), White (B), Green (C), Fuchsia (D) and Yellow (E)

Cast on with A. K 2 rows.

Work 22 rows of Blossom Chart.

Cont as desired.

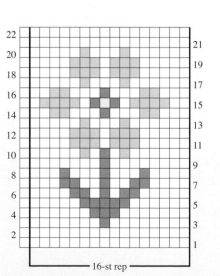

16-st rep

Color Key

- A
- B
- C
- D
- E

wrap bow

(over 38 sts)

• If desired, cont 4-row ribbon on each side.

Colors Black (A), Light Pink (B) and Dark Pink (C)

Cast on with A. K 2 rows.

Work 18 rows of Wrap Bow Chart.

Cont as desired.

Color Key
- A
- B
- C

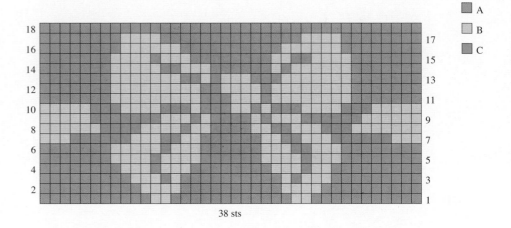

38 sts

lucky charms

(multiple of 22 sts plus 14)

Colors White (A) and Green (B)

Cast on with A. K 2 rows.

Work 13 rows of Lucky Charms Chart.

Cont as desired.

Color Key
- A
- B

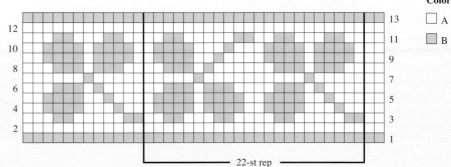

22-st rep

bow

(multiple of 38 sts plus 2)

Colors Dark Pink (A), White (B) and Light Pink (C)

Cast on with A. K 2 rows.

Work 14 rows of Bow Chart.

Cont as desired.

■ A

□ B

■ C

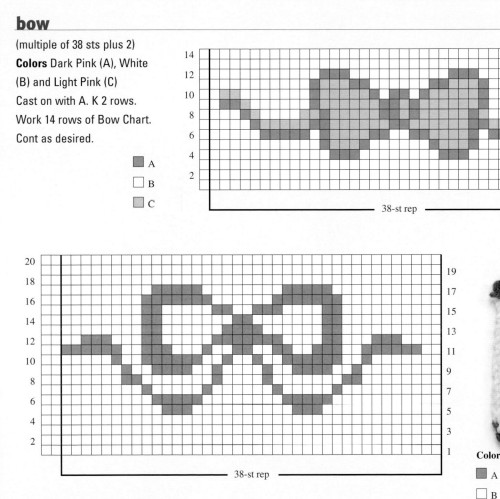

38-st rep

11-st rep

garland bow

(multiple of 38 sts plus 2)

Colors Pink (A) and White (B)

Cast on with A. K 2 rows.

Work 20 rows of Garland Bow Chart.

Cont as desired.

Color Key

■ A

□ B

clover repeats

(multiple of 11 sts plus 3)

Colors White (A) and Green (B)

Cast on with A. K 2 rows.

Work 14 rows of Clover Repeats Chart.

Cont as desired.

Color Key

□ A

■ B

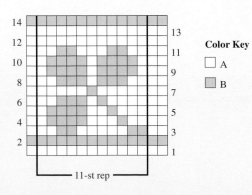

spring flowers

(multiple of 12 sts plus 1)

Colors Yellow (A), White (B), Olive Green (C) and Orange (D)

Cast on with A. K 2 rows.

Work 12 rows of Spring Flowers Chart.

Cont as desired.

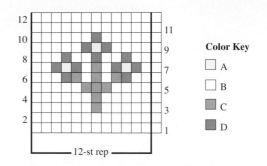

Color Key

☐ A
☐ B
■ C
■ D

12-st rep

royal florals

(multiple of 36 sts plus 1)

Colors Purple (A), White (B), Black (C), Orange (D), Dark Pink (E), Yellow (F), Lavender (G) and Light Pink (H)

Cast on with A. K 2 rows.

Work 13 rows of Royal Florals Chart.

Cont as desired.

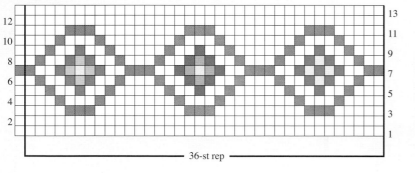

36-st rep

Color Key

■ A
☐ B
■ C
■ D
■ E
☐ F
■ G
☐ H

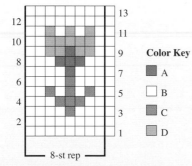

Color Key

■ A
☐ B
■ C
■ D

8-st rep

tulips

(multiple of 8 sts plus 1)

Colors Purple (A), White (B), Green (C) and Lavender (D)

Cast on with A. K 2 rows.

Work 13 rows of Tulips Chart.

Cont as desired.

papillon

(multiple of 14 sts plus 3)

Colors Purple (A), White (B), Gray (C), Black (D) and Lavender (E)

Cast on with A. K 2 rows.

Work 16 rows of Papillon Chart.

Cont as desired.

Embroider French Knots and Straight St.

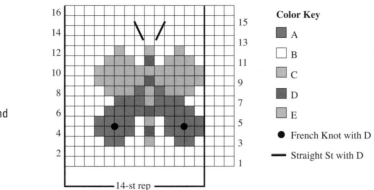

Color Key
- A
- B
- C
- D
- E
- ● French Knot with D
- — Straight St with D

14-st rep

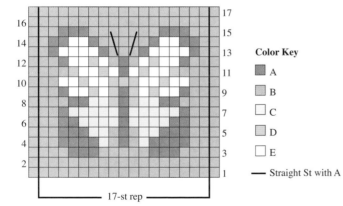

Color Key
- A
- B
- C
- D
- E
- — Straight St with A

17-st rep

butterfly

(multiple of 17 sts plus 2)

Colors Black (A), Gray (B), Light Yellow (C), Gold (D) and White (E)

Cast on with A. K 2 rows.

Work 17 rows of Butterfly Chart.

Cont as desired.

moon phases

(multiple of 36 sts plus 2)

Colors Blue (A), Yellow (B) and Gold (C)

Cast on with A. K 2 rows.

Work 15 rows of Moon Phases Chart.

Cont as desired.

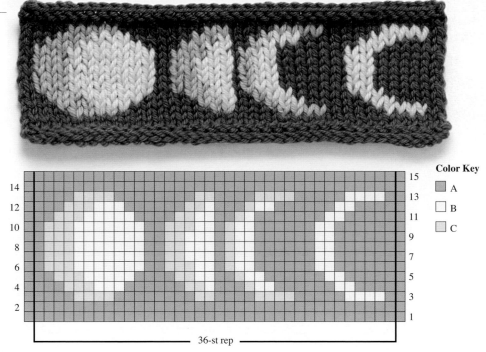

Color Key

A
B
C

36-st rep

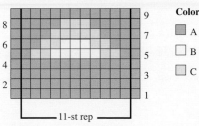

Color Key

A
B
C

11-st rep

sunset

(multiple of 11 sts plus 2)

Colors Blue (A), Yellow (B) and Gold (C)

Cast on with A. K 2 rows.

Work 9 rows of Sunset Chart.

Cont as desired.

sun (with 2 ray variations)

(multiple of 13 sts plus 2)

Colors Blue (A), Yellow (B) and Gold (C)

Cast on with A. K 2 rows.

Work 16 rows of Sun Chart.

Cont as desired.

With B, embroider desired ray pattern with Straight St.

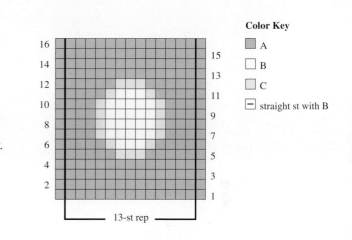

Color Key

- A
- B
- C
- — straight st with B

13-st rep

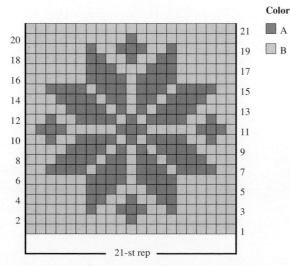

21-st rep

Color Key

- A
- B

scandinavian snowflake

(multiple of 21 sts)

Colors Blue (A) and Gray (B)

Cast on with A. K 4 rows.

Work 21 rows of Scandinavian Snowflake Chart.

Cont as desired.

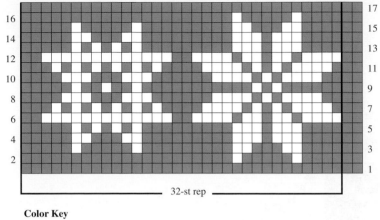

classic snowflake

(multiple of 32 sts plus 2)

Colors White (A) and Blue (B)

Cast on with A. K 2 rows.

Work 17 rows of Classic Snowflake Chart.

Cont as desired.

Color Key

☐ A

▨ B

open snowflake outline

(multiple of 18 sts plus 1)

Colors Gray (A) and Blue (B)

Cast on with A. K 4 rows.

Work 19 rows of Open Snowflake Outline Chart.

Cont as desired.

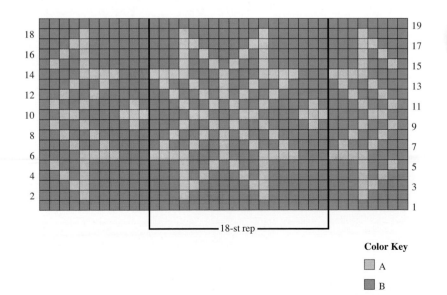

Color Key

▨ A

▨ B

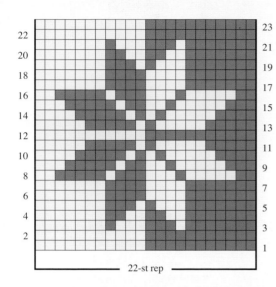

22-st rep

boxed 2-color snowflake

(multiple of 22 sts)

Colors Blue (A) and Yellow (B)

Note Bring new color under old at color change to twist yarns and prevent holes.

Cast on with A.

Next row (RS) *K11A, k11B; rep from * to end.

Next row *K11B, k11A; rep from * to end.

Work 24 rows of Boxed 2-Color Snowflake Chart.

Cont as desired.

2-color snowflake

(multiple of 21 sts)

Colors Blue (A) and Green (B)

Cast on with A. K 4 rows.

Work 22 rows of 2-Color Snowflake Chart.

Cont as desired.

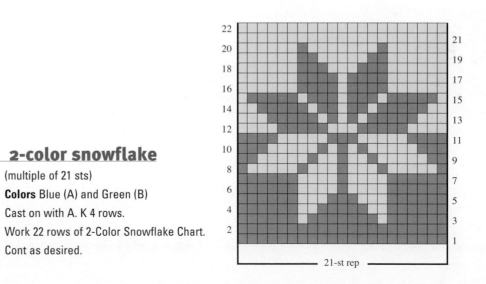

21-st rep

spruce tree

(multiple of 14 sts plus 13)

Colors Olive (A) and White (B)

Cast on with A. K 2 rows.

Work 20 rows of Spruce Tree Chart.

Cont as desired.

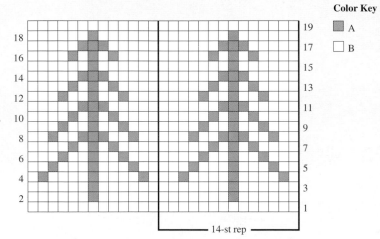

Color Key

A

B

14-st rep

Color Key

A

B

pine tree

(multiple of 11 sts plus 2)

Colors Olive (A) and White (B)

Cast on with A. K 2 rows.

Work 16 rows of Pine Tree Chart.

Cont as desired.

11-st rep

tree tops

(multiple of 12 sts plus 1)

Colors Olive (A), White (B) and Gold (C)

Cast on with A. K 2 rows.

Work 20 rows of Tree Tops Chart.

Cont as desired.

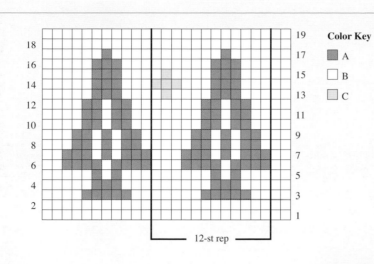

Color Key
- A
- B
- C

12-st rep

starbright

(multiple of 13 sts)

Colors Blue (A), White (B) and Red (C)

Cast on with A. Work 5 rows in St st. K 1 row on WS for turning ridge.

Work 19 rows of Starbright Chart.

Cont as desired.

Fold hem to WS at turning ridge and sew in place.

Color Key
- A
- B
- C

13-st rep

small stars

(multiple of 8 sts plus 3)

Colors Blue (A) and Yellow (B)

Cast on with A. K 2 rows.

Work 11 rows of Small Stars Chart.

Cont as desired.

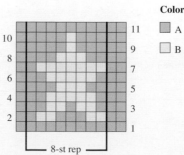

Color Key
- A
- B

8-st rep

sitting duck

(multiple of 14 sts plus 2)

Colors Blue (A), Yellow (B), Gold (C) and Black (D)

Cast on with A. K 2 rows.

Work 16 rows of Sitting Duck Chart.

Cont as desired.

Embroider French Knot.

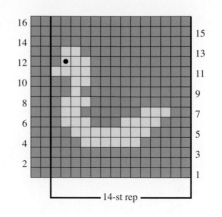

14-st rep

waves

(multiple of 7 sts plus 1)

Colors Dark Blue (A) and Light Blue (B)

Cast on with A. K 2 rows.

Work 11 rows of Waves Chart.

Cont as desired.

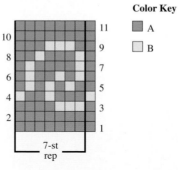

7-st rep

fishy

(multiple of 34 sts plus 2)

Colors Blue (A), Gold (B), Olive Green (C), Black (D) and White (E)

Cast on with A. K 2 rows.

Work 12 rows of Fishy Chart.

Cont as desired.

Embroider French Knots.

Color Key

- A
- B
- C
- ● French knot with D
- ○ French knot with E

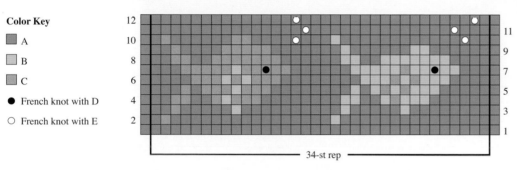

34-st rep

boys and girls

(multiple of 16 sts plus 3)

Colors Blue (A) and Gold (B)

Cast on with A. K 2 rows.

Work 18 rows of Boys and Girls Chart.

Cont as desired.

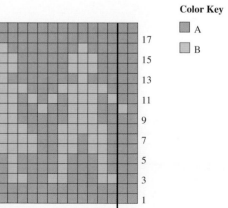

Color Key

- A
- B

16-st rep

fleur de lys I

(multiple of 40 sts plus 1)
Colors Purple (A) and Gold (B)
Cast on with A.
Work 30 rows of Fleur de Lys I Chart.
Cont as desired.

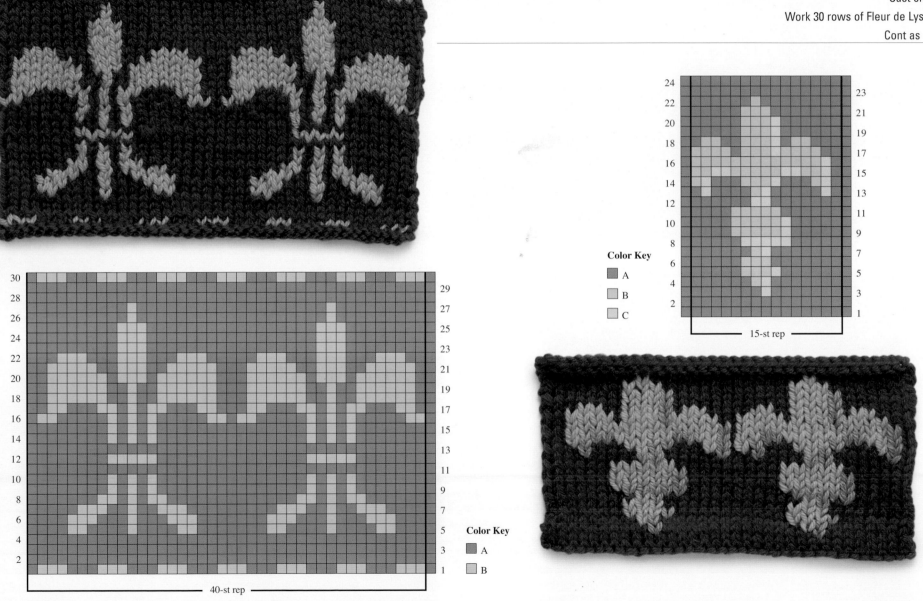

Color Key
- A
- B
- C

15-st rep

Color Key
- A
- B

40-st rep

fleur de lys III

(multiple of 23 sts plus 3)

Colors: Blue (A) and Gold (B)

Cast on with A. K 2 rows.

Work 24 rows of Fleur de Lys III Chart.

Cont as desired.

fleur de lys II

(multiple of 15 sts plus 2)

Colors Purple (A), Gold (B) and Gray (C)

Cast on with A. Work 5 rows in St st. K 1 row on WS for turning ridge.

Work 24 rows of Fleur de Lys II Chart.

Cont as desired.

Fold hem to WS at turning ridge and sew in place.

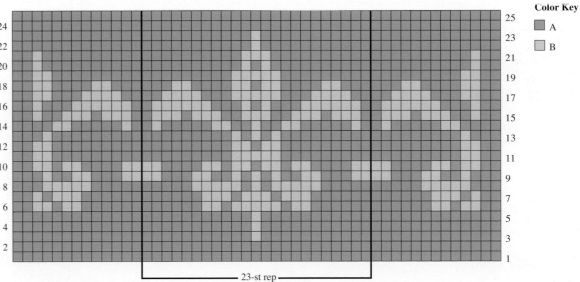

Color Key

- A
- B

23-st rep

leopard spots

(multiple of 33 sts plus 4)

Colors Light Gold (A), Black (B) and Dark Gold (C)

Cast on with A. K 2 rows.

Work 16 rows of Leopard Spots Chart.

Cont as desired.

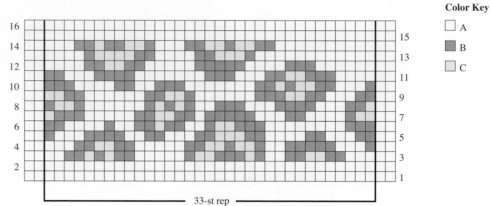

Color Key

☐ A
◼ B
☐ C

33-st rep

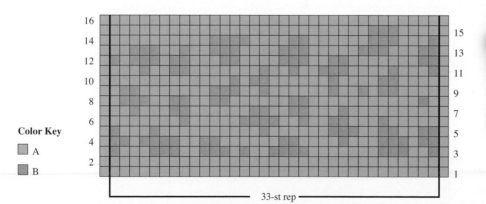

Color Key

◼ A
◼ B

33-st rep

cheetah spots

(multiple of 33 sts plus 2)

Colors Brown (A) and Black (B)

Cast on with A. Work 5 rows in St st. K 1 row on WS for turning ridge.

Work 16 rows of Cheetah Spots Chart.

Cont as desired.

Fold hem to WS at turning ridge and sew in place.

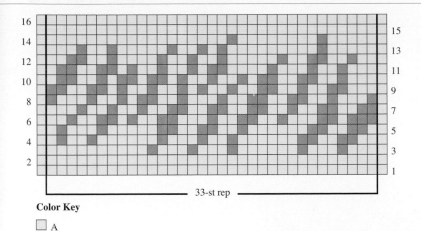

tiger stripes

(multiple of 33 sts plus 2)

Colors Gold (A) and Black (B)

Cast on with A. Work 5 rows in St st.

K 1 row on WS for turning ridge.

Work 16 rows of Tiger Stripes Chart.

Cont as desired.

Fold hem to WS at turning ridge and sew in place.

Color Key

☐ A

▨ B

giraffe spots

(multiple of 28 sts plus 2)

Colors Gold (A) and Brown (B)

Cast on with A. Work 5 rows in St st.

K 1 row on WS for turning ridge.

Work 16 rows of Giraffe Spots Chart.

Cont as desired.

Fold hem to WS at turning ridge and sew in place.

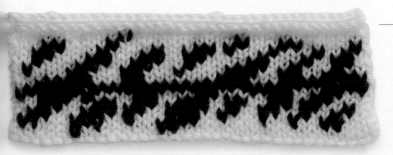

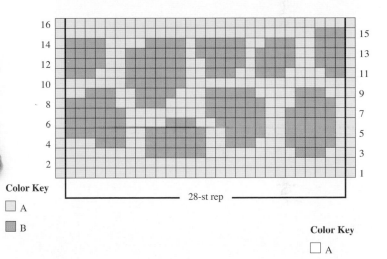

Color Key

☐ A

▨ B

Color Key

☐ A

▨ B

zebra stripes

(multiple of 33 sts plus 2)

Colors White (A) and Black (B)

Cast on with A. Work 5 rows in St st.

K 1 row on WS for turning ridge.

Work 16 rows of Zebra Stripes Chart.

Cont as desired.

Fold hem to WS at turning ridge and sew in place.

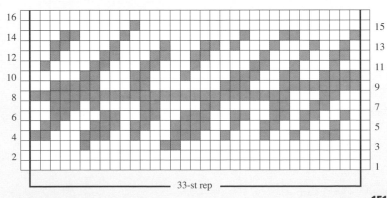

starburst

(multiple of 12 sts plus 3)

Colors Blue (A), Dark Pink (B), Yellow (C) and Lavender (D)

Cast on with A. K 2 rows.

Work 12 rows of Starburst Chart.

Cont as desired.

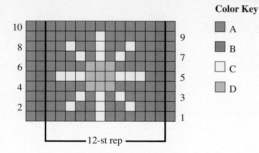

Color Key

- ■ A
- ■ B
- ☐ C
- ■ D

12-st rep

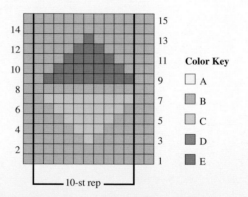

Color Key

- ☐ A
- ■ B
- ☐ C
- ■ D
- ■ E

10-st rep

2-faced diamonds

(multiple of 10 sts plus 3)

Colors Yellow (A), Lavender (B), Light Green (C), Blue (D) and Red (E)

Cast on with A. K 2 rows.

Work 15 rows of 2-Faced Diamonds Chart, working diamonds with colors A, C, D and E, as desired.

Cont as desired.

dots

(multiple of 10 sts plus 1)

Colors Lavender (A), Blue (B), Light Green (C), Red (D) and Yellow (E)

Cast on with A.

Work Seed st

Rows 1 and 3 (RS) *K1, p1; rep from *, end k1.

Rows 2 and 4 (WS) Rep row 1.

Work 12 rows of Dots Chart, using B for dots and background, and A, C, D or E for "frame" around dot.

Cont as desired.

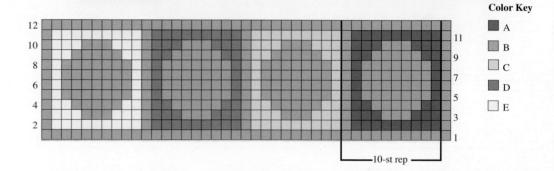

Color Key
- A
- B
- C
- D
- E

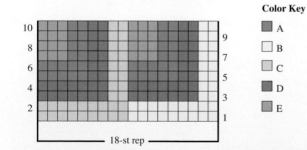

Color Key
- A
- B
- C
- D
- E

log cabins

(multiple of 18 sts)

Colors Lavender (A), Yellow (B), Green (C), Red (D) and Blue (E)

Cast on with A. K 2 rows.

Work 10 rows of Log Cabins Chart.

Cont as desired.

nouveau

links

▶ ▲ (beg with 8 sts and end with multiple of 24 sts)

• Each link requires 2 strips which are worked separately, then all links are joined on the same row.

• Cut yarn on all but last strip and leave sts on needle.

Cast on 8 sts.

Work in St st for 4"/10cm.

Cut yarn and leave sts on needle. On same needle, cast on and work as above to make another strip. Cont in this manner until desired number of strips are made (2 strips are required for each hooked loop).

To join links *K8, bring first strip in back of second strip, fold second strip to back catching the first strip, using 3-needle joining technique (see page 188), k8 from second strip tog with 8 sts picked up from cast-on edge, k8 from cast on edge of first strip; rep from * to last strip.

Row 1 (WS) Purl.

Row 2 *K1, p1; rep from * to end.

Row 3 *P1, k1; rep from * to end.

Cont until desired length.

twisted loops

▶ ▲ (beg with 6 sts and end with multiple of 12 sts)

• Each loop is worked separately, then all loops are joined on the same row.

• Cut yarn on all but last strip and leave sts on needle.

• Alternate colors as desired.

Cast on 6 sts.

Work in St st for 3"/8cm.

Cut yarn and leave sts on needle. On same needle, cast on and work as above to make another strip. Cont in this manner until desired number of strips are made (each strip makes 12 sts).

To join links

*K6, bring cast on edge of first strip behind second strip, using 3-needle joining technique (see page 188) k6 from second strip tog with 6 sts picked up from cast-on edge; rep from * to last strip, k6 from cast on edge of last strip.

Purl 1 row.

Cont as desired.

cable knots

▶ ▲ (beg with 8 sts and end with a multiple of 18 sts)

• Each knot requires 2 strips which are worked separately, then all knots are joined on the same row.

• Cut yarn on all but last strip and leave sts on needle.

Cast on 8 sts.

Work in St st for 4"/10cm.

Cut yarn and leave sts on needle. On same needle, cast on and work as before to make another strip. Cont in this manner until desired number of strips are made.

To join

Cast on 1 st, *cross cast on end of first strip over second strip. Bring cast on end of second strip between both strips and hold behind sts on needle of first strip, [k1 from first strip, k1 from first strip at the same time picking up and knitting 1 st from cast on edge of second strip] 4 times. Turn, cast on 1 st, turn.

Bring cast-on end of first strip behind sts on needle of second strip, [k1 from second strip, k1 from second strip at the same time picking up and knitting 1 st from cast-on edge of first strip] 4 times. Turn, cast-on 1 st, turn.

Rep from * to last strip.

Cont as foll:

Rows 1, 3, 5, 7 and 9 (WS) K2, *p6, k3; rep from *, end k2.

Rows 2, 6 and 8 P2, *k6, p3; rep from *, end p2.

Row 4 K1, p1, *Sl sts sts to cn and hold to front, k3, k3 from cn, p3, Sl 3 sts to cn and hold to back, k3, k3 from cn, p3; rep from *, end p1, k1.

Cont as desired.

hook loops

▶ ▲ (beg with 8 sts and end with multiple of 16 sts)

• Each loop is worked separately, then all loops are joined on the same row.

• Cut yarn on all but last strip and leave sts on needle.

• Alternate colors as desired.

Cast on 8 sts.

Work in St st for 4"/10cm.

Cut yarn and leave sts on needle. On same needle, cast on and work as before to make another strip. Cont in this manner until desired number of strips are made (each strip makes 16 sts).

To join links

*K8, bring cast on edge of first strip behind second strip, using 3-needle joining technique (see page 188) k8 from second strip tog with 8 sts picked up from cast on edge; rep from * to last strip, k8 from cast on edge of last strip.

Purl 1 row.

Cont as desired.

garter cups

▶ ▲ (beg with 7 sts and end with multiple of 14 sts)

• Each cup is worked separately, then all cups are joined on the same row.

• Cut yarn on all but last cup and leave sts on needle.

Cast on 7 sts.

Work in garter st for 3"/7.5cm.

Cut yarn and leave sts on needle. On same needle, cast on and work as before to make another strip. Cont in this manner until desired number of strips are made (each strip makes 14 sts).

To join cups

*K7, with RS facing, k7 from cast on edge; rep from * to last strip.

Cont as desired.

rib cups

▶ ▲ (beg with 8 sts and end with multiple of 16 sts)

• Each cup is worked separately, then all cups are joined on the same row.

• Cut yarn on all but last cup and leave sts on needle.

Cast on 8 sts.

Row 1 (RS) *K1, p1; rep from * to end.

Rep row 1 for 3"/7.5cm.

Cut yarn and leave sts on needle. On same needle, cast on and work as before to make another strip. Cont in this manner until desired number of strips are made (each strip makes 16 sts).

To join cups

*K8, with RS facing, k8 from cast-on edge; rep from * to last strip.

Cont as desired.

garter cups reversed

rib cups reversed

queen's ball

▼ Cast on 8 sts, leaving a long tail for seaming.

Row 1 *K into front and back of every st—16 sts.

Row 2 and all WS rows Purl.

Rows 3, 5, 7 and 9 Knit.

Row 11 *K2tog; rep from * to end—8 sts.

With tapestry needle run thread through 8 sts and gather, securing thread. Thread cast-on tail and run through cast-on sts and gather, securing thread. Stuff with polyfil. Sew side edges together. Attach or hang from any edge.

king's ball

▲ Cast on 10 sts, leaving a long tail for seaming.

Row 1 *K into front and back of every st—20 sts.

Row 2 and all WS rows Purl.

Rows 3, 5, 7, 9 and 11 Knit.

Row 13 *K2tog; rep from * to end—10 sts.

Row 14 *P2tog; rep from * to end—5 sts.

With dpn work St st cord (see page 188) for desired length. Place on holder. Cont in this manner until desired number of balls are made, alternating lengths of cords as desired.

With tapestry needle run thread through cast-on sts and gather, securing thread. Stuff with poly fill. Sew side edges together.

To join balls, *K5 cord sts, turn, cast on 5 sts, turn; rep from * to end. Cont as desired.

rib flaps

▲ (multiple of 8 sts)

• Each flap is worked separately, then all flaps are joined on the same row.

• Break yarn on all but last flap and leave sts on needle.

• Alternate colors as desired.

Cast on 8 sts.

Work in k1, p1 rib for desired length.

Break yarn and leave sts on needle. On same needle, cast on and work as above to make another flap. Cont in this manner until desired number of flaps are made. To join flaps, *K1, p1; rep from * across all flaps on needle.

Cont as desired.

fur ball

▼ Cast on 4 sts.

Row 1 *K into front and back of every st— 8 sts.

Row 2 and all WS rows Purl.

Rows 3, 5 and 7 Knit.

Row 9 *K2tog; rep from * to end.

Row 11 Pass 2nd, 3rd, 4th st over 1st stitch.

Fasten off, leaving a long enough tail for sewing. Sew side edges together. Stuff with polyfil. Thread tail through 4 cast-on sts, pull tightly and secure. Sew or hang from any edge.

garter stitch ball

▼ (multiple of 10 sts plus 5, one ball required for each multiple)

Row 1 (RS) Knit.

Row 2 *K5, p5; rep from *, end k5.

Rep rows 1 and 2 until desired length.

Cont as desired.

To make balls

Cast on 9 sts, leaving a long tail for seaming.

Work in garter st for 2.5"/6cm.

Bind off so tail is on the same side as cast-on tail. Using a tail, sew cast-on edge to bound-off edge, secure yarn. Thread tail through edge sts, gather and secure, do not cut tail. Stuff with polyfil. Thread rem tail through rem edge sts, gather and secure. Cont in this manner until desired number of balls are made. Tie tails to middle st of each St st rib.

button flap

▶ ▲ (multiple of 10 sts)

• Each flap is worked separately, then all flaps are joined on the same row.

• Break yarn on all but last flap and leave sts on needle.

**Cast on 9 sts.

Row 1 *K1, p1; rep from *, end k1.

Rep row 1 for 4"/10cm.

Break yarn and leave sts on needle. On same needle, cast on and work as above to make another flap. Cont in this manner until desired number of flaps are made.

To join flaps, *work 9 sts from 1 flap on LH needle, cast on 1 st; rep from * to last flap, k9. Cont in seed st or as desired.**

Fold flaps to RS and sew on button.

crossed flap

▶ ▲ (multiple of 10 sts)

• Each flap is worked separately in alternating colors, then all flaps are joined on the same row.

• Break yarn on all but last flap and leave sts on needle.

Work from ** to ** of button flap.

Sew cast on edge of first flap behind second flap. Repeat across all flaps. Sew last flap into seam.

knotted flap

▶ ▲ (multiple of 10 sts)

• Each flap is worked separately, then all flaps are joined on the same row.

• Break yarn on all but last flap and leave sts on needle.

Work from ** to ** of Button Flap.

Knot end of each or alternating flap as desired.

garter short flaps

(multiple of 8 sts)

• Each flap is worked separately, then all flaps are joined on the same row.

• Break yarn on all but last flap and leave sts on needle.

Cast on 8 sts.

Work in garter st for 1"/2.5cm.

Break yarn and leave sts on needle. On same needle, cast on and work as above to make another flap. Cont in this manner until desired number of flaps are made.

To join flaps, knit across all flaps on needle.

Cont in garter st or as desired.

openwork ladder

▼ ▶ ▲ (multiple of 8 sts plus 5)

Work 8 rows in garter st.

Row 1 (RS) *Bind off 5 sts, k until there are 3 sts from bind-off, leave rem sts on spare needle.

Work in garter st on these 3 sts for 2"/5cm. Break yarn, placing sts on holder. Rejoin yarn and rep from * to last 5 sts, bind off.

Row 2 Cast on 5 sts to RH needle, *k the next 3 sts, turn, cast on 5 sts, turn; rep from * to end.

K 8 rows.

Cont as desired.

open work x's

▼ ▶ ▲ (multiple of 16 sts plus 5)

Work 8 rows in garter st.

Row 1 (RS) *Bind off 5 sts, k until there are 3 sts from bind-off, leave rem sts on holder.

Work in garter st on these 3 sts for 2"/5cm. Break yarn, leaving sts on needle. Rejoin yarn and rep from * to last 5 sts, bind off.

Row 2 Cast on 5 sts to RH needle, *sl 3 sts from LH needle to cable needle and hold in back, k3 from LH needle, cast on 5 sts on RH needle, k3 from cable needle, cast on 5 sts on RH needle; rep from * to last strip, end cast on 5 sts.

Work 8 rows in garter st.

Bind off.

layered garter short flaps

▶ ▲ (multiple of 8 sts)

• Each flap is worked separately, then all flaps are joined on the same row.

• Break yarn on all but last flap and leave sts on needle.

First layer

Cast on 8 sts.

Work in garter st for 1"/2.5cm.

Break yarn and leave sts on needle. On same needle, cast on and work as above to make another flap. Cont in this manner until desired number of flaps for first layer are made.

To join flaps, knit across all flaps on needle. Work 9 rows in garter st. Leave sts on spare needle.

Second layer

Cast on 4 sts and knit for 1"/2.5cm (for ½ flap). Break yarn and leave sts on needle. Make flaps as before, making one less flap, end with another ½ flap.

To join layers, place needle with 2nd layer over first with RS facing. Using 3-needle joining technique (see page 188) knit sts from layers together.

Cont in garter st or as desired.

spaced garter short flaps

▶ ▲ (multiple of 11 sts plus 8)

• Each flap is worked separately, then all flaps are joined on the same row.

• Break yarn on all but last flap and leave sts on needle.

Cast on 8 sts.

Work in garter st for 1"/2.5cm.

Break yarn and leave sts on needle. On same needle, cast on and work as above to make another flap. Cont in this manner until desired number of flaps are made.

To join flaps, *K8, turn, cast on 3 sts, turn; rep from * to last flap, k8.

Cont in garter st or as desired.

southern flare

▶ Cast on 25 sts.

Row 1 (RS) Sl 1, k19, yo, p2tog, k1, yo, k2.

Row 2 K4, yo, p2tog, k18, turn.

Row 3 Sl 1, k17, yo, p2tog, k2, yo, k2.

Row 4 K5, yo, p2tog, k16, turn.

Row 5 Sl 1, k15, yo, p2tog, k3 yo, k2.

Row 6 K6, yo, p2tog, k14, turn.

Row 7 Sl 1, k13, yo, p2tog, k2tog, yo twice, k2, yo, k2.

Row 8 K6, p1, k1, yo, p2tog, k12, turn.

Row 9 Sl 1, k11, yo, p2tog, k8.

Row 10 Bind off 5 sts, k2, yo, p2tog, k10, turn.

Row 11 Sl 1, k9, yo, p2tog, k1, yo, k2.

Row 12 K4, yo, p2tog, k8, turn.

Row 13 Sl 1, k7, yo, p2tog, k2, yo, k2.

Row 14 K5, yo, p2tog, k6, turn.

Row 15 Sl 1, k5, yo, p2tog, k3, yo, k2.

Row 16 K6, yo, p2tog, k4, turn.

Row 17 Sl 1, k3, yo, p2tog, k2tog, yo twice, k2, yo, k2.

Row 18 K6, p1, k1, yo, p2tog, k2, turn.

Row 19 Sl 1, k1, yo, p2tog, k8.

Row 20 Bind off 5 sts, k2, yo, p2tog, k2, [yo, k2tog] 8 times, k2.

Rep rows 1 to 20 until desired length. Bind off on the 20th row. Run ribbon through eyelet holes.

amulet

▲ (multiple of 19 sts)

RT K2tog leaving sts on LH needle, then k first st again, sl both sts off needle.

LT K the second st tbl, then k the first st and sl both sts off needle.

Increase Right (inc R) Insert RH needle downward into the back of the st in the row below the next st on LH needle (i.e., into the purled head of st on the back of the fabric), and knit; then knit the st on LH needle in the usual way.

Increase Left (inc L) Knit (from front) into the st in the row below the next st on LH needle; then knit the st on LH needle in the usual way.

Knit 2 rows.

Row 1 (WS) K6, [p1, k1] 3 times, p1, k6.

Row 2 P5, RT, [k1, p1] twice, k1, LT, p5.

Row 3 K5, p2, [k1, p1] 3 times, p1, k5.

Row 4 P4, RT, [p1, k1] 3 times, p1, LT, p4.

Row 5 K4, [p1, k1] 5 times, p1, k4.

Row 6 P3, RT, [k1, p1] twice, [k1, p1, k1] in next st, [p1, k1] twice, LT, p3.

Row 7 K3, p2, k1, p1, k1, p5, k1, p1, k1, p2, k3.

Row 8 P2, RT, [p1, k1] twice, p1, inc R, k1, inc L, p1, [k1, p1] twice, LT, p2.

Row 9 K2, [p1, k1] 3 times, p7, [k1, p1] 3 times, k2.

Row 10 P2, k1tbl, [k1, p1] 3 times, inc R, k3, inc L, [p1, k1] 3 times, k1tbl, p2.

Row 11 K2, [p1, k1] 3 times, p9, [k1, p1] 3 times, k2.

Row 12 P2, k1tbl, [k1, p1] 3 times, k2, S2KP, k2, [p1, k1] 3 times, k1tbl, p2.

Row 13 Rep row 9.

Row 14 P2, k1tbl, [k1, p1] 3 times, k1, S2KP, k1, [p1, k1] 3 times, k1tbl, p2.

Row 15 K2, [p1, k1] 3 times, p5, [k1, p1] 3 times, k2.

Row 16 P2, k1tbl, [k1, p1] 3 times, S2KP, [p1, k1] 3 times, k1tbl, p2.

Row 17 K2, [p1, k1] 3 times, p3, [k1, p1] 3 times, k2.

Row 18 P2, LT, p1, k1, p1, RT, k1, LT, p1, k1, p1, RT, p2.

Row 19 K3, p2, k1, [p3, k1] twice, p2, k3.

Row 20 P3, LT, k1, RT, p1, k1, p1, LT, k1, RT, p3.

Work in seed st for 1"/2.5cm. Cont as desired.

Cut 3 lengths each approx 8"/20.5cm long for each fringe (see page 17). Attach groups of 3 to bottom of each amulet.

holsters

▲ (multiple of 4 sts plus 4)

Work 4 rows in garter st.

Row 1 (RS) P4, *turn, cast on 8 sts, turn, p4; rep from * to end.

Row 2 K4, *p8, k4; rep from * to end.

Row 3 P4, *k8, p4; rep from * to end.

Rows 4, 6 and 8 Rep row 2.

Rows 5, 7 and 9 Rep row 3.

Row 10 K4, *bind off 8 sts purlwise, k4; rep from * to end.

Row 11 Purl.

Row 12 Knit.

Cont as desired.

open tubes

▲ (multiple of 3 sts plus 3)

Work 2 rows in garter st.

Row 1 (RS) P3, *turn, cast on 5 sts, turn, p3; rep from * to end.

Row 2 K3, *5, k3; rep from * to end.

Row 3 P3, *k5, p3; rep from * to end.

Rows 4, 6, 8, 10, 12 and 14 Rep row 2.

Rows 5, 7, 9, 11, 13 and 15 Rep row 3.

Row 16 K3, *bind off 5 sts purlwise, k3; rep from * to end.

Row 17 Purl.

Row 18 Knit.

Cont as desired.

staggered holsters

▲ (multiple of 4 sts plus 4)

Work 4 rows in garter st.

Work rows 1 to 12 of Holsters.

Row 13 P6, *turn, cast on 8 sts, turn, p4; rep from * end k2.

Row 14 K6, *p8, k4; rep from * end k2.

Row 15 P6, *k8, p4; rep from * end p2.

Rows 16, 18 and 20 Rep row 14.

Rows 17, 19 and 21 Rep row 15.

Row 22 K6, *bind off 8 sts in p, k4; rep from * end k2.

Row 23 Purl.

Row 24 Knit.

Cont as desired.

holsters reversed

staggered holsters reversed

t twist ruffle

▲ (multiple of 6 sts)

• Cast on 2 times the number of sts needed for edging that is a multiple of 6.

Work 6 rows in St st.

Next row (RS) K6, then rotate the LH needle counter-clockwise 360 degrees, then k another 6 sts and rotate the LH needle again counter-clockwise 360 degrees. Cont to k6 sts and rotate LH needle, to the end of the row. Cont in St or desired pattern until desired length, end with a WS row.

Next (dec) row *K2tog; rep from * to end.

Cont as desired.

open scallop ruffle

▲ (beg with multiple of 11 sts plus 2 and end with multiple of 4 sts)

Row 1 (WS) Purl.

Row 2 K2, *k1 and sl st back to LH needle, with RH needle, lift next 8 sts, 1 at a time, over this st and off needle, yo twice, k the first st again, k2; rep from * to end.

Row 3 K1, *p2 tog, drop first yo of previous row, [k1, p1, k1, p1] in second yo (4 sts), p1; rep from *, end k1.

Work in St st for desired ruffle length.

Next row (RS) *k2tog; rep from * to end.

Cont as desired.

holey ruffle

▼ (beg with multiple of 3 st plus 3 and end with multiple of 6 sts plus 3) ▶◀

Work 4 rows in garter st.

Row 1 (RS) P3, *turn, cast on 6 sts, turn, p3; rep from * to end.

Row 2 K3, *p6, k3; rep from * to end.

Row 3 P3, k6, p3; rep from * to end.

Rows 4, 6, 8, 10 and 12 Rep row 2.

Rows 5, 7, 9 and 11 Rep row 3.

Bind off.

holey ruffle reversed

diamond gym

▲ (multiple of 16 sts)

Work 2 rows in garter st.

Row 1 (RS) *K2, p3, 2/1 RPC, 2/1 LPC, p3, k2; rep from * to end.

Row 2 *P2, k3, p2, k2, p2, k3, p2; rep from * to end.

Row 3 *K2, p2, 2/1 RPC, p2, 2/1 LPC, p2, k2; rep from * to end.

Row 4 *P2, k2, p2, k4, p2, k2, p2; rep from * to end.

Row 5 *K2, p1, 2/1 RPC, p4, 2/1 LPC, p1, k2; rep from * to end.

Row 6 *P2, k1, p2, k6, p2, k1, p2; rep from * to end.

Row 7 *K2, 2/1 RPC, p6, 2/1 LPC, k2; rep from * to end.

Row 8 *P4, k8, p4; rep from * to end.

Row 9 *2/2 LC, p8, 2/2 RC; rep from * to end.

Row 10 Rep row 8.

Row 11 *K2, 2/1 LPC, p6, 2/1 RPC, k2; rep from * to end.

Row 12 Rep row 6.

Row 13 *K2, p1, 2/1 LPC, p4, 2/1 RPC, p1, k2; rep from * to end.

Row 14 Rep row 4.

Row 15 *K2, p2, 2/1 LPC, p2, 2/1 RPC, p2, k2; rep from * to end.

Row 16 Rep row 2.

Row 17 *K2, p3, 2/1 LPC, 2/1 RPC, p3, k2; rep from * to end.

Row 18 *P2, k4, p4, k4, p2; rep from * to end.

Row 19 *K2, p4, 2/2 RC, p4, k2; rep from * to end.

Row 20 Rep row 18.

Cont as desired.

x's

▲ (multiple of 16 sts)

Work 2 rows in garter st.

Row 1 (RS) *K2, 2/1 RPC, p6, 2/1 LPC, k2; rep from * to end.

Row 2 *P4, k8, p4; rep from * to end.

Row 3 *2/2 LC, p8, 2/2 RC; rep from * to end.

Row 4 Rep row 2.

Row 5 *K2, 2/1 LPC, p6, 2/1 RPC, k2; rep from * to end.

Row 6 *P2, k1, p2, k6, p2, k1, p2; rep from * to end.

Row 7 *K2, p1, 2/1 LPC, p4, 2/1 RPC, p1, k2; rep from * to end.

Row 8 *P2, k2, p2, k4, p2, k2, p2; rep from * to end.

Row 9 *K2, p2, 2/1 LPC, p2, 2/1 RPC, p2, k2; rep from * to end.

Row 10 *P2, k3, p2, k2, p2, k3, p2; rep from * to end.

Row 11 *K2, p3, 2/1 LPC, 2/1 RPC, p3, k2; rep from * to end.

Row 12 *P2, k4, p4, k4, p2; rep from * to end.

Row 13 *K2, p4, 2/2 RC, p4, k2; rep from * to end.

Row 14 Rep row 12.

Row 15 *K2, p3, 2/1 RPC, 2/1 LPC, p3, k2; rep from * to end.

Row 16 Rep row 10.

Row 17 *K2, p2, 2/1 RPC, p2, 2/1 LPC, p2, k2; rep from * to end.

Row 18 Rep row 8.

Row 19 *K2, p1, 2/1 RPC, p4, 2/1 LPC, p1, k2; rep from * to end.

Row 20 Rep row 6.

Cont as desired.

x cables

▲ (multiple of 24 sts plus 20)

Work 2 rows in garter st.

Row 1 (RS) P2, *2/2 RC, p8, 2/2 LC, p8; rep from *, end last rep p2.

Row 2 K2, *p4, k8, p4, k8; rep from *, end last rep k2.

Row 3 P2, *k2, 2/2 LPC, p4, 2/2 RPC, k2, p8; rep from *, end last rep p2.

Row 4 K2, *p2, k2, p2, k4, p2, k2, p2, k8; rep from *, end last rep k2.

Row 5 P2, *k2, p2, 2/2 LPC, 2/2 RPC, p2, k2, p8; rep from *, end last rep p2.

Row 6 K2, *p2, k4, p4, k4, p2, k8; rep from *, end last rep k2.

Row 7 P2, *k2, p4, 2/2 LC, p4, k2, p8; rep from *, end last rep p2.

Row 8 Rep row 6.

Row 9 P2, *k2, p2, 2/2 RPC, 2/2 LPC, p2, k2, p8; rep from *, end last rep p2.

Row 10 Rep row 4.

Row 11 P2, *k2, 2/2 RPC, p4, 2/2 LPC, k2, p8; rep from *, end last rep p2.

Row 12 Rep row 2.

Row 13 P2, *2/2 LC, p8, 2/2 RC, p8; rep from ˣ, end last rep p2.

Row 14 Rep row 2.

Row 15 P2, *k4, p8, k4, p8; rep from *, end last rep p2.

Row 16 Rep row 2.

Row 17 Rep row 13.

Row 18 Rep row 2.

Cont as desired.

layered sea scallops

▲ (multiple of 14 sts)

• Each scallop is worked separately in alternating colors, then all scallops are joined on the same row.

• Cut yarn on all but last scallop and leave sts on needle.

First layer

Cast on 5 sts.

Row 1 Knit.

Row 2 Yo, knit to end.

Rep row 2 until there are 14 sts.

Knit 2 rows.

Cut yarn and leave sts on needle. On same needle, cast on and work as before to make another scallop. Cont in this manner until desired number of scallops for first layer are made, leaving sts on spare needle.

Second layer

Left ½ scallop Cast on 3 sts.

Row 1 Knit.

Row 2 Yo, knit to end.

Row 3 Knit.

Rep rows 2 and 3 until there are 7 sts. Cut yarn and leave sts on needle. Make scallops as for first layer, making one less scallop.

Right ½ scallop Work as for left scallop, reversing shaping.

To join layers, place needle with 2nd layer over first with RS facing. Using 3-needle joining technique (see page 188) knit sts from layers together.

Cont in garter st or as desired.

bobble v's

▲ (multiple of 23 sts)

MB (make bobble) [K1, yo, k1] in st, turn, p3, turn, sl 1, k2tog, psso.

3/2 RPC Sl next 2 sts to cn and hold to back, k3, p2 from cn.

3/2 LPC Sl next 3 sts to cn and hold to front, p2, k3 from cn.
Knit 1 row.

Row 1 (WS) *K8, p7, k8; rep from * to end.

Row 2 *P6, 3/2 RPC, k1tbl, 3/2 LPC, p6; rep from * to end.

Row 3 *K6, p4, k1, p1, k1, p4, k6; rep from * to end.

Row 4 *P6, k1, MB, k1, [k1tbl, p1] 2 times, k1tbl, k1, MB, k1, p6; rep from * to end.

Row 5 *K6, p4, k1, p1, k1, p4, k6; rep from * to end.

Row 6 *P4, 3/2 RPC, [k1tbl, p1] 2 times, k1tbl, 3/2 LPC, p4; rep from * to end.

Row 7 *K4, p4, [k1, p1] 3 times, k1, p4, k4; rep from * to end.

Row 8 *P4, k1, MB, k1, [k1tbl, p1] 4 times, k1tbl, k1, MB, k1, p4; rep from * to end.

Row 9 *K4, p4, [k1, p1] 3 times, k1, p4, k4; rep from * to end.

Row 10 *P2, 3/2 RPC, [k1tbl, p1] 4 times, k1tbl, 3/2 LPC, p2; rep from * to end.

Row 11 Knit.

Cont as desired.

royal diamonds

▲ (multiple of 16 sts plus 17)

Cluster 5—K next 5 sts and slip them onto cable needle. Wrap yarn 4 times counter-clockwise around these 5 sts, then slip sts back onto RH needle.

MB (make bobble) K in front, back, front and back again all in next st—4 sts, turn, k4, turn, p4. With LH needle, lift 2nd, 3rd, and 4th sts over first st—1 st.
Knit 1 row.

Row 1 (WS) K6, p2, k1, p2, *k11, p2, k1, p2; rep from * to last 6 sts, k6.

Row 2 P6, cluster 5, *p11, cluster 5; rep from * to last 6 sts, p6.

Row 3 Rep row 1.

Row 4 P4, p2tog, k2, M1 p-st, p1, M1 p-st, k2, p2tog, *p7, p2tog, k2, M1 p-st, p1, M1 p-st, k2, p2tog; rep from * to last 4 sts, p4.

Row 5 K5, p2, k3, p2, *k9, p2, k3, p2; rep from * to last 5 sts, k5.

Row 6 P3, p2tog, k2, M1 p-st, p3, M1 p-st, k2, p2tog, *p5, p2tog, k2, M1 p-st, p3, M1 p-st, k2, p2tog; rep from * to last 3 sts, p3.

Row 7 K4, p2, k5, p2, *k7, p2, k5, p2; rep from * to last 4 sts, k4.

Row 8 P2, p2tog, k2, M1 p-st, p5, M1 p-st, k2, p2tog, *p3, p2tog, k2, M1 p-st, p5, M1 p-st, k2, p2tog; rep from * to last 2 sts, p2.

Row 9 K3, p2, k7, p2, *k5, p2, k7, p2; rep from * to last 3 sts, k3.

Row 10 P1, *p2tog, k2, M1 p-st, p7, M1 p-st, k2, p2tog, p1; rep from * to end.

Row 11 K2, p2, k9, p2, *k3, p2, k9, p2; rep from * to last 2 sts, k2.

Row 12 P2tog, k2, M1 p-st, p9, *M1 p-st, k2, p3tog, k2, M1 p-st, p9; rep from * to last 4 sts, M1 p-st, k2, p2tog.

Row 13 K1, *p2, k11, p2, k1; rep from * to end.

Row 14 P1, k2, p5, MB, p5, *cluster 5, p5, MB, p5; rep from * to last 3 sts, k2, p1.

Row 15 Rep row 13.

Row 16 P1, *M1 p-st, k2, p2tog, p7, p2tog, k2, M1 p-st, p1; rep from * to end.

Row 17 K2, p2, k9, p2, *k3, p2, k9, p2; rep from * to last 2 sts, k2.

Row 18 P2, M1 p-st, k2, p2tog, p5, p2tog, k2, M1 p-st, *p3, M1 p-st, k2, p2tog, p5, p2tog, k2, M1 p-st; rep from * to last 2 sts, p2.

Row 19 K3, p2, k7, p2, *k5, p2, k7, p2; rep from * to last 3 sts, k3.

Row 20 P3, M1 p-st, k2, p2tog, p3, p2tog, k2, M1 p-st, *p5, M1 p-st, k2, p2tog, p3, p2tog, k2, M1 p-st; rep from * to last 3 sts, p3.

Row 21 K4, p2, k5, p2, *k7, p2, k5, p2; rep from * to last 4 sts, k4.

Row 22 P4, M1 p-st, k2, p2tog, p1, p2tog, k2, M1 p-st, *p7, M1 p-st, k2, p2tog, p1, p2tog, k2, M1 p-st; rep from * to last 4 sts, p4.

Row 23 K5, p2, k3, p2, *k9, p2, k3, p2; rep from * to last 5 sts, k5.

Row 24 P5, M1 p-st, k2, p3tog, k2, M1 p-st, *p9, M1 p-st, k2, p3tog, k2, M1 p-st; rep from * to last 5 sts, p5.

Row 25 Purl.

Cont as desired.

Cut and trim tassels.

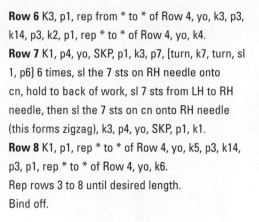

ribbon candy

▶ Cast on 36 sts.

Row 1 (WS) Knit.

Row 2 Knit.

Row 3 K1, yo, SKP, p5, k3, p14, k3, yo, SKP, p5, k1.

Row 4 K5, p1, *sl st just purled to LH needle, pass next st on LH needle over and sl the st back to RH needle*, yo, k1, p3, k7, [turn, p7, turn, sl 1, k6] 6 times, sl the 7 sts from RH needle onto cn and hold to front of work, sl 7 sts from LH to RH needle, then sl the 7 sts from the cn onto RH needle (this forms zigzag), p3, k4, p1, rep from * to *, yo, k2.

Row 5 K1, p2, yo, SKP, p3, k3, p14, k3, p2, yo, SKP, p3, k1.

Row 6 K3, p1, rep from * to * of Row 4, yo, k3, p3, k14, p3, k2, p1, rep * to * of Row 4, yo, k4.

Row 7 K1, p4, yo, SKP, p1, k3, p7, [turn, k7, turn, sl 1, p6] 6 times, sl the 7 sts on RH needle onto cn, hold to back of work, sl 7 sts from LH to RH needle, then sl the 7 sts on cn onto RH needle (this forms zigzag), k3, p4, yo, SKP, p1, k1.

Row 8 K1, p1, rep * to * of Row 4, yo, k5, p3, k14, p3, p1, rep * to * of Row 4, yo, k6.

Rep rows 3 to 8 until desired length.

Bind off.

ribbon candy B

▶ Cast on 18 sts.

Row 1 (WS) Knit.

Row 2 Knit.

Row 3 K2, p14, k2.

Row 4 P2, k7, [turn, p7, turn, sl 1, k6] 6 times, sl the 7 sts from RH needle onto cn and hold to front of work, sl 7 sts from LH to RH needle, then sl the 7 sts from the cn onto RH needle (this forms zigzag), p2.

Row 5 K2, p14, k2.

Row 6 P2, k14, p2.

Row 7 K2, p7, [turn, k7, turn, sl 1, p6] 6 times, sl the 7 sts on RH needle onto cn, hold to back of work, sl 7 sts from LH to RH needle, then sl the 7 sts on cn onto RH needle (this forms zigzag), k2.

Row 8 Rep row 6.

Rep rows 3 to 8 until desired length.

Bind off.

twisted garter strips

▶ **First half**

Cast on 15 sts.

**Work 6 rows in garter st.

Next row (RS) K11, (place rem sts on a holder).

Next row (WS) K1, p10.

Rep last 2 rows over these 11 sts 8 times more.

Place sts on second holder, do not cut yarn.

Slip 4 sts from first holder to needle, join a new ball of yarn and work 32 rows in garter st. Cut yarn and place sts on first holder.

Second half

Cast on 15 sts. Work 6 rows in garter st.

Next row (RS) K4, place rem 11 sts on third holder.

Work 31 rows in garter st. Place sts on fourth holder, do not cut yarn.

Slip 11 sts from third holder to needle, join a new ball of yarn, knit to end of row.

Next row (WS) P10, k1.

Next row Knit.

Rep last 2 rows 7 times more, then first row once.

Break yarn and place sts on third holder.

Next row (RS) K11 sts from first half (second holder), twist the two garter st strips around each other as shown in photo, then k4 from the first half (first holder); then using the ball from the 2nd half, k4 sts from the second half (fourth holder), k11 sts from second half (third holder).

Working 15 sts of each half separately, cont in St st and garter st as established for 7 rows.**

Repeat from ** to **.

Cont until desired length.

Bind off each half separately.

butterfly bowtie

▲ (multiple of 12 sts plus13)

Row 1 (RS) Purl.

Row 2 Knit.

Row 3 P3, *[k1, p1, k1] in next st, p5, [k1, p1, k1] in next st, p5; rep from *, end last rep p3.

Row 4 K3, *p3, k5, p3, k5; rep from *, end last rep k3.

Row 5 P3, *k2, SKP, p3, k2tog, k2, p5; rep from *, end last rep p3.

Row 6 K3, *p3, k3, p3, k5; rep from *, end last rep k3.

Row 7 P3, *k2, SKP, p1, k2tog, k2, p5; rep from *, end last rep p3.

Rows 8 and 10 K3, *p3, k1, p3, k5; rep from *, end last rep k3.

Row 9 P3, *sl next 7 sts to cn and wrap yarn clockwise around these 7 sts twice, sl sts to LH needle, k3, p1, k3, p5; rep from *, end last rep with p3.

Row 11 P3, *k3, M1p-st, p1, M1p-st, k3, p5; rep from *, end last rep with p3.

Row 12 K3, *p3, k3, p3, k5; rep from *, end last rep k3.

Row 13 P3, * k3, M1p-st, p1, insert LH needle into corresponding st from row 5 and k it tog with next st on needle, p1, M1p-st, k3, p5; rep from *, end last rep with p3.

Row 14 K3, *p3, k5, p3, k5; rep from *, end last rep k3.

Row 15 P3, *SK2P, p1, [insert LH needle into corresponding st from row 13 and k it tog with next st on needle, p1] twice, SK2P, p5; rep from *, end last rep p3.

Row 16 Knit.

Cont as desired.

bella knot fringe

▶ **3/1 RPC** Sl 1 st to cn and hold to back, k3, p1 from cn.

3/1 LPC Sl 3 sts to cn and hold to front, p1, k3 from cn.

3/3 RPC Sl 3 sts to cn and hold to back, k3, p3 from cn.

3/3 LPC Sl 3 sts to cn and hold to front, p3, k3 from cn.

3/3 RC Sl 3 sts to cn and hold to back, k3, k3 from cn.

3/3 LC Sl 3 sts to cn and hold to front, k3, k3 from cn.

Cast on 28 sts.

Row 1 (WS) K7, p3, k13, p3, k2.

Row 2 P2, 3/1 LPC, p11, 3/1 RPC, p7.

Row 3 K8, p3, k11, p3, k3.

Row 4 P3, 3/1 LPC, p4, M1, p1 in front, back and front of next st, M1, p4, 3/1 RPC, p8.

Row 5 K9, p3, k4, p2, [p1, yo, p1] in next st, p2, k4, p3, k4.

Row 6 P4, 3/1 LPC, 3/3 RPC, p1, 3/3 LPC, 1/3 RPC, p9.

Row 7 K10, p6, k7, p6, k5.

Rows 8, 12 and 16 P5, 3/3 RC, p7, 3/3 LC, p10.

Rows 9, 11, 13, 15 and 17 K10, p6, k7, p6, k5.

Rows 10 and 14 P5, k6, p7, k6, p10.

Row 18 P4, 3/1 RPC, 3/3 LC, p1, 3/3 RC, 3/1 LPC, p9.

Row 19 K9, p3, k4, dec 6 sts over next 7 sts as follows: slip 4 wyif, [pass 2nd st on RH needle over 1st st (center st), slip center st back to LH needle, pass 2nd st on LH needle over center st, slip center st back to RH needle] 3 times. Slip center st to LH and k it, k4, p3, k4.

Row 20 P3, 3/1 RPC, p9, 3/1 LPC, p8.

Row 21 K8, p3, k11, p3, k3.

Row 22 P2, 3/1 RPC, p11, 3/1 LPC, p7.

Row 23 K7, p3, k13, p3, k2.

Row 24 P2, k3, p13, k3, p7.

Rep rows 1 to 24 until desired length, end with a WS row.

Bind off 22 sts, fasten off 23rd st. Sl rem 5 sts off needle and unravel them on every row for fringe. Cut loops and trim.

queen anne's lace

▶ Cast on 20 sts.

Row 1 (RS) Sl 1, k1, [yo, k2tog] 4 times, p3, k2tog, yo, k3, yo, k2.

Row 2 Yo, k2tog, k19.

Row 3 Sl 1, k2, [yo, k2tog] 3 times, p3, k2tog, yo, k5, yo, k2.

Row 4 Yo, k2tog, k20.

Row 5 Sl 1, k1, [yo, k2tog] 3 times, p3, k2tog, yo, [k2tog] twice, yo 3 times, k2tog, k1, yo, k2.

Row 6 Yo, k2tog, k3, work (k1, p1, k1) in triple yo, k15.

Row 7 Sl 1, k2, [yo, k2tog] 3 times, p3, k1, yo, k2tog, k3, k2tog, yo, k2tog, k1.

Row 8 Yo, k2tog, k20.

Row 9 Sl 1, k1, [yo, k2tog] 4 times, p3, k1, yo, k2tog, k1, k2tog, yo, k2tog, k1.

Row 10 Yo, k2tog, k19.

Row 11 Sl 1, k2, [yo, k2tog] 4 times, p3, k1, yo, SK2P, yo, k2tog, k1.

Row 12 Yo, k2tog, k18.

Rep rows 1 to 12 until desired length.

Bind off.

partridge

▶ Cast on 16 sts.

Row 1 (RS) K6, M1, k2tog, M1, k2tog, yo 4 times, k2tog, k1, M1, k2tog, k1.

Row 2 K2, p4, k1, p1, k1, p2, k1, p1, k6.

Row 3 K2, M1, k2tog, k3, M1, k2tog, M1, k2tog, k4, k2tog, M1, k2.

Row 4 K2, p8, k1, p1, k7.

Row 5 K2, k2tog, yo twice, k2tog, k2, M1, k2tog, M1, k2tog, k3, k2tog, M1, k2.

Row 6 K2, p7, k1, p1, k4, p1, k3.

Row 7 K2, M1, k2tog, k5, M1, k2tog, M1, k2tog, k2, k2tog, M1, k2.

Row 8 K2, p6, k1, p2, k8.

Row 9 K2, k2tog, yo twice, k2tog, k4, M1, k2tog, M1, k2tog, k1, k2tog, M1, k2.

Row 10 K2, p5, k1, p3, k4, p1, k3.

Row 11 K2, M1, k2tog, k7, M1, k2tog, M1, (k2tog) twice, M1, k2.

Row 12 K2, p4, k1, p4, k8.

Row 13 K12, M1, k2tog, M1, k2tog, k3.

Row 14 Bind off 3 sts, p1, k1, p5, k8.

Rep rows 1 to14 until desired length.

Bind off.

poplar

▶ Cast on 9 sts.

Row 1 (WS) K3, p4, [p1, k1] into next st, p1.

Row 2 SK2P, yo, SKP, yo, k1tbl, yo, k2tog, k2.

Row 3 K3, p4, [p1, k1] into next st, p1.

Row 4 SK2P, yo, k1tbl, [yo, k3] twice.

Row 5 K3, p6, [p1, k1] into next st, p1.

Row 6 SK2P, yo, k1tbl, yo, k2tog, k1, SKP, yo, k3.

Row 7 K3, p6, [p1, k1] into next st, p1.

Row 8 SK2P, yo, k1tbl , yo, k2tog, k1, SKP, yo, k3.

Row 9 K3, p6, [p1, k1] into next st, p1.

Row 10 SK2P, yo, SKP, yo, SK2P, yo, k2tog, k2.

Repeat rows 1 to 10 until desired length.

Bind off.

toggle knot

▶ **3/1 LPC** Slip 3 sts to cn and hold in front, p1, k3 from cn.

2/3 RPC Sl 2 st to cn and hold in back, k3, p2 from cn.

lpdd P2tog, return resulting st to LH needle, then pass next st over it and off needle, then sl the st back to RH needle.

rpdd Sl 1, p2tog tbl, then pass the sl st over the p2tog and off needle.

3/3 RC Sl 3 sts to cn and hold in back, k3, k3 from cn.

3/3 LC Sl 3 st to cn and hold in front, k3, k3 from cn.

Cast on 27 sts.

Row 1 (WS) P1, k1, p1, k9, p3, k9, p1, k1, p1.

Row 2 K1, p1, k1, p4, k into front, back and front of next st, p4, k3, p9, k1, p1, k1.

Row 3 P1, k1, p1, k9, p3, k4, p3, k4, p1, k1, p1.

Row 4 K1, p1, k1, p4, 3/1 LPC, p3, k3, p9, k1, p1, k1.

Row 5 P1, k1, p1, k9, p3, k3, p3, k5, p1, k1, p1.

Row 6 K1, p1, k1, p5, 3/1 LPC, p2, k3, p6, k into front, back and front of next st, p2, k1, p1, k1.

Row 7 P1, k1, p1, k2, p3, k6, p3, k2, p3, k6, p1, k1, p1.

Row 8 K1, p1, k1, p6, 3/1 LPC, p1, k3, p4, 2/3 RPC, p2, k1, p1, k1.

Row 9 P1, k1, p1, k4, p3, k4, p3, k1, p3, k7, p1, k1, p1.

Row 10 K1, p1, k1, p7, 3/1 LPC, k3, p2, 2/3 RPC, p4, k1, p1, k1.

Row 11 P1, k1, p1, k6, p3, k2, p6, k8, p1, k1, p1.

Row 12 K1, p1, k1, p8, 3/3 RC, 2/3 RPC, p6, k1, p1, k1.

Row 13 P1, k1, p1, k8, p9, k8, p1, k1, p1.

Row 14 K1, p1, k1, p8, k3, 3/3 LC, p8, k1, p1, k1.

Row 15 P1, k1, p1, k8, p9, k8, p1, k1, p1.

Row 16 K1, p1, k1, p8, 3/3 RC, k3, p8, k1, p1, k1.

Row 17 P1, k1, p1, k8, p9, k8, p1, k1, p1.

Row 18 K1, p1, k1, p6, 2/3 RPC, 3/3 LC, p8, k1, p1, k1.

Row 19 P1, k1, p1, k8, p6, k2, p3, k6, p1, k1, p1.

Row 20 K1, p1, k1, p4, 2/3 RPC, p2, k3, 3/1 LPC, p7, k1, p1, k1.

Row 21 P1, k1, p1, k7, p3, k1, p3, k4, p3, k4, p1, k1, p1.

Row 22 K1, p1, k1, p2, 2/3 RPC, p4, k3, p1, 3/1 LPC, p6, k1, p1, k1.

Row 23 P1, k1, p1, k6, p3, k2, p3, k6, rpdd, k2, p1, k1, p1.

Row 24 K1, p1, k1, p9, k3, p2, 3/1 LPC, p5, k1, p1, k1.

Row 25 P1, k1, p1, k5, p3, k3, p3, k9, p1, k1, p1.

Row 26 K1, p1, k1, p9, k3, p3, 3/1 LPC, p4, k1, p1, k1.

Row 27 P1, k1, p1, k4, lpdd, k4, p3, k9, p1, k1, p1.

Row 28 K1, p1, k1, p9, k3, p9, k1, p1, k1.

Rep rows 1 to 28 for desired length.

Bind off.

zig-zag and bobbles

▶ **Ltw2** Sl next st to cn and hold at front, p1, k1 from cn wrapping around needle twice. On the foll row, drop the extra wrap.

MB K1, p1, k1, p1, k1 in next st, turn, k5, turn, p5, pass 2nd, 3rd, 4th and 5th sts over 1 st.

Cast on 18 sts.

Row 1 (WS) P2, [k1, p1] 5 times, p1, k5.

Row 2 K5, k1tbl, [Ltw2] 3 times, p5, k1tbl.

Row 3 P1, k5, [p1, k1] 3 times, p1, k5.

Row 4 K5, k1tbl, p1, [Ltw2] 3 times, p2, MB, p1, k1tbl.

Row 5 P1, k4, [p1, k1] 3 times, k1, p1, k5.

Row 6 K5, k1tbl, p2, [Ltw2] 3 times, p3, k1bl.

Row 7 P1, k3, [p1, k1] 3 times, k2, p1, k5.

Row 8 K5, k1tbl, p3, [Ltw2] 3 times, p2, k1tbl.

Row 9 P1, k2, [p1, k1] 3 times, k3, p1, k5.

Row 10 K5, k1bl, p1, MB, p2, [Ltw2] 3 times, p1, k1tbl.

Row 11 P1, k1, [p1, k1] 3 times, k4, p1, k5.

Row 12 K5, k1tbl, p5, [Ltw2] 3 times, k1bl.

Rep rows 1 to 12 until desired length, end with a RS row.

Bind off 12 sts and fasten off 13th st. Slip rem 5 sts off needle and unravel them on every row for fringe.

tied daisy stitch

▲ (worked over multiple of 10 sts plus 1 extra)
K 6 rows before beginning pat.

Row 1 (WS) K5, *[bring yarn from back to front and around right hand needle to back] 3 times (triple yo), k1, work triple yo, k9; repeat from *, end last rep k5.

Row 2 K across row, sl all yos from left hand needle and hold to front.

Tie daisies Insert free needle into each pair of loops and pull up snugly, holding thumb and forefinger of left hand at base of loops, to take the slack out of sts between and on either side of this pair of loops. Tie each pair of loops into a single knot. Rep rows 1 and 2, pull up loops taking out slack but do not tie. Rep rows 1 and 2 once more. Pull up loops and again tie these in a single knot (this will make a total of 3 pairs of loops in a vertical line in each motif across row).

To form daisies Tie upper right loop and lower left loop into a single knot. Tie upper left loop and lower right loop into a single knot. Tie middle pair of loops into a firm square knot across the 2 single knots just tied. Tie each group (3 pairs of loops) in this manner across row. Knit next 12 rows (6 ridges on RS of fabric between daisy rows). End with RS row.

Row 3 K10, *triple yo, k1, triple yo, k9; rep from *, end k1.

Row 4 Rep row 2. Pull up loops and tie in a single knot. Rep rows 3 and 4, pull up loops taking out slack, but do not tie. Rep rows 3 and 4 once more, pull up loops and tie in a single knot. (This will make a total of 3 pairs of loops in each motif across row as before.)

Tie loops to form daisies.

Knit 12 rows.

Rep these 38 rows for desired length.

cookie twist

▲ (multiple of 16 sts plus 8)

Work in garter st for 3 rows.

Row 1 (RS) K8, *sl next 8 sts on holder, turn, cast on 8 sts, turn, k8; rep from * to end.

Row 2 Purl.

Cont in St st for 2"/5 cm. Leave sts on needle, do not cut yarn.

*With second ball of yarn, k8 from holder and work in St st for 2¼"/5.5cm. Cut yarn and place on holder; rep from * across sts on holder.

Next row K8, *with WS facing, twist 8 sts on holder counterclockwise once, using 3-needle joining technique (see page 188) k8 from holder and needle together, k8; rep from * to end.

Cont as desired.

Sew cast on sts to twist sts on WS.

hot wheels scallops

▶ ▲ • Worked with 2 needle sizes and 2 yarns. Large needle size should be 4 sizes larger than small needle size.

• Hot wheels scallops can be sewn to any edge with small needles and ply yarn. With smaller needles and ply or DK yarn, cast on 12 sts.

Work 5 rows in garter st.

Change to mohair and larger needles.

Row 3 *K into front and back of every st—24 sts.

Rows 4, 6, 8, 10 and 12 Purl

Rows 5, 7, 9, and 11 Knit.

Change to smaller needles and ply or DK yarn.

Row 13 *K2tog; rep from * to end—12 sts

Work 5 rows in garter st.

Bind off.

Fold in half with WS tog and slip st edges together. Make desired number of wheels. Sew wheels to any edge.

multi-ball tassel

▲ See page 160. Stack and attach as many balls together as desired.

tinker bells

▲ (multiple of 13 sts)

MB K1, p1, k1, p1, k1 in next st, with LH needle lift 2nd, 3rd, 4th and 5th sts over first st—1 st.

C9B Sl 5 sts to cn and hold in back, k4, k5 from cn.

DD Sl 2 sts tog knitwise, k1, pass 2 slip sts over k st—2 sts dec.

Row 1 (WS) Knit.

Row 2 *P2, k9, p2; rep from * to end.

Row 3 and all WS rows *K2, p9, k2; rep from * to end.

Row 4 *P2, yo, SKP, k5, k2tog, yo, p2; rep from * to end.

Row 6 *P2, k1, yo, SKP, k3, k2tog, yo, k1, p2; rep from * to end.

Row 8 *P2, MB, k1, yo, SKP, k1, k2tog, yo, k1, MB, p2; rep from * to end.

Row 10 *P2, k1, MB, k1, yo, DD, yo, k1, MB, k1 p2; rep from * to end.

Row 12 *P2, k2, MB, k3, MB, k2, p2; rep from * to end.

Row 14 *P2, k3, MB, k1, MB, k3, p2; rep from * to end.

Row 16 *P2, k4, MB, k4, p2; rep from * to end.

Rows 18, 20, 22 *P2, k9, p2; rep from * to end.

Row 24 *P2, C9B, p2; rep from * to end.

Row 26 Purl.

Cont as desired.

yo yos

▲ Worked with 2 needle sizes and 2 yarns. Large needle size should be 4 sizes larger than small needle size.

With smaller needles and ply or DK yarn, cast on 12 sts, leaving an 8"/20cm tail for seaming.

Row 1 Knit.

Row 2 Purl.

Change to mohair and larger needles.

Row 3 *K into front and back of every st—24 sts.

Rows 4, 6, 8 and 10 Purl.

Rows 5, 7 and 9 Knit.

Change to smaller needles and ply or DK yarn.

Row 11 *K2tog; rep from * to end—12 sts.

Row 12 Purl.

Bind off.

Cut yarn, leaving an 8"/20cm tail. Sew side edges together. Thread bind off tail through bound-off sts, pull tight to form circle, and secure. Thread cast on tail through cast on sts, and repeat. Sew yo-yos evenly spaced to any edge.

jester's points

▲ (multiple of 27 sts plus 15)

• Each point is worked separately, then all points are joined on the same row.

• Cut yarn on all but last point and leave sts on needle.

MB K1, p1, k1, p1, k1 in next st, [turn, k5] 4 times, pass 2nd, 3rd, 4th and 5th sts over first st.

Cast on 2 sts.

Row 1 (RS) Knit.

Row 2 Yo, knit to end—3 sts.

Row 3 Yo, knit to end—4 sts.

Row 4 Yo, knit to end—5 sts.

Row 5 Yo, knit to end—6 sts.

Row 6 Yo, knit to end—7 sts.

Row 7 Yo, knit to end—8 sts.

Row 8 Yo, knit to end—9 sts.

Row 9 Yo, knit to end—10 sts.

Row 10 Yo, knit to end—11 sts.

Row 11 Yo, knit to end—12 sts.

Row 12 Yo, knit to end—13 sts.

Row 13 Yo, knit to end—14 sts.

Row 14 Yo, knit to end—15 sts.

Cut yarn and leave sts on needle.

On same needle, cast on and work rows 1 to 11 (12 sts) to make another point. Cont in this manner until desired number of points are made, ending with 15 st point and leaving sts on spare needle.

To join flaps, knit across sts of all points on needle.

Work 2 rows in garter st.

Next row (RS) K2, *MB, k5; rep from *, end last rep k3.

Work 5 rows in garter st.

Cont as desired.

p a t t e r n s

UNIQUE RIBS
BOBBLE RIB FLOWER PULLOVER

SIZES

To fit Small (Medium, Large). Directions are for smaller size with larger sizes in parentheses. If there is only one figure, it applies to all sizes.

KNITTED MEASUREMENTS

- Bust 38½ (42½, 45½)"/98 (108, 115.5)cm
- Length 20 (21, 22)"/51 (53.5, 56)cm
- Upper arm 15½ (16¾, 18)"/39.5 (42.5, 45.5)cm

MATERIALS

- 7 (8, 9) 1¾oz/50g balls (each approx 124yd/113m) of Classic Elite *Lush* (angora/wool) in #4441 Red (MC) ④
- 1 ball each in #4434 Plum (A), #4402 Olive (B), #4413 Black (C), #4468 Rust (D), #4474 Light Green (E) and #4457 Blue (F)
- One pair each sizes 7 and 8 (4.5 and 5mm) needles OR SIZE TO OBTAIN GAUGE
- Size 7 (4.5mm) circular needle, 16"/40cm long
- Two size 6 (4mm) dpn
- Tapestry needle

GAUGES

- 20 sts and 24 rows = 4"/10cm over Bobble Rib using smaller needles.
- 16 sts and 24 rows = 4"/10cm over St st using larger needles.

TAKE TIME TO CHECK GAUGES.

STITCH GLOSSARY

MB make bobble ([K1, p1] 2 times) in same st, turn, p4, turn, k4, pass 2nd 3rd 4th and 5th st over first st—1 st rem.

Bobble rib

(multiple of 5 sts plus 2)

Rows 1, 3 and 7 P2, *k3, p1; rep from * to end.

Rows 2, 4, 6 and 8 K the knit sts and p the purl sts.

Row 5 P2, *k1, MB, k1, p2; rep from * to end.

Rep rows 1 to 8 for bobble rib.

Bobble in chart

Knit into front, back, front and back of st. Turn. P4, turn, k4, turn, p4, turn, k2tog twice. Turn, p2tog—1 st rem.

Note Bobbles in center of flower can be knit in as above or worked separately and attached later (see FINISHING).

BACK

With smaller needles and MC, cast on 57 (67, 72) sts. Work in Bobble Rib for 8"/20.5cm, ending with a RS row. Change to larger needles and p next row on WS, inc 14 (12, 13) sts evenly across row—71 (79, 85) sts.

Beg chart

Work stripe and Fair Isle pat from chart (rows 1 to 11) omitting flower stem, then work to end with MC, AT THE SAME TIME, inc 1 st each side every 4th row 3 times—77 (85, 91) sts. Work even in St st and MC until piece measures 11½ (12, 12½)"/29 (30.5, 32)cm from beg.

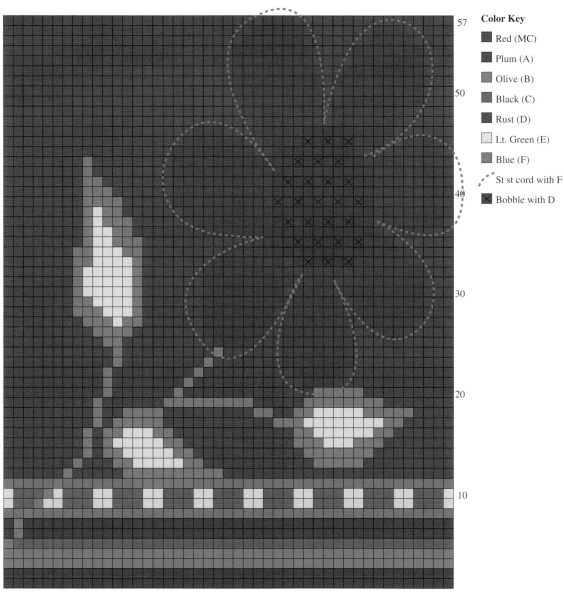

Color Key

- ■ Red (MC)
- ■ Plum (A)
- ■ Olive (B)
- ■ Black (C)
- ■ Rust (D)
- □ Lt. Green (E)
- ■ Blue (F)
- ⌇ St st cord with F
- ⊠ Bobble with D

45 sts

Armhole shaping

Bind off 4 (5, 6) sts at beg of next 2 rows, 2 sts at beg of next 2 rows, 1 st at beg of next 2 rows—63 (69, 73) sts. Work even until armhole measures 8½ (9, 9½)"/21.5 (23, 24)cm. Bind off.

FRONT

Work as for back (including all shaping) but work chart above bobble rib as foll: **Next row (RS)** Work 8 (12, 15) sts A, work row 1 of chart over 45 sts, work with A to end. Cont in this way, working sts outside of chart in colors corresponding to chart, and after all chart rows have been worked, cont with MC only to end of piece. After armhole shaping has been worked, work even until armhole measures 6½ (7, 7½)"/16.5 (17.5, 19)cm, ending with a WS row.

Neck Shaping

Next row (RS) K20 (23, 25) sts, join a 2nd ball of yarn and bind off center 23 sts, k to end. Working both sides at once, bind off 2 sts at each neck edge once, then dec 1 st at each neck edge once—17 (20, 22) sts rem for each shoulder. When piece measures same as back to shoulder, bind off sts each side.

SLEEVES

With smaller needles and MC, cast on 42 (47, 52) sts. Work bobble rib for 10"/25.5cm, ending with a WS row. Change to larger needles and p next row on WS, inc 10 sts evenly across row—52 (57, 62) sts.

Beg chart

Work stripe and Fair Isle pat from chart (rows 1 to 11) omitting flower stem, then work to end with MC, AT THE SAME TIME, inc 1 st each side every 4th row 5 times—62 (67, 72) sts.

Cont in St st until sleeve measures 17 (17, 17½)"/43 (43, 44.5)cm from beg, ending with a WS row.

Cap shaping

Bind off 4 (5, 6) sts at the beg of next 2 rows, 2 sts at beg of next 2 rows, 1 st at beg of

next 2 rows. Work even for 6 (6, 8) rows. Dec 1 st each side every other row 6 (7, 8) times, *every* row 6 times. Bind off 3 sts at beg of next 6 rows. Bind off rem 6 (7, 8) sts.

FINISHING

Weave in all loose ends. Block very lightly to measurements, leaving rib to pull in. Sew shoulder seams.

Collar

With circular needle and MC and with RS facing, pick up and knit 90 sts evenly around neck. Join and pm to mark beg of rnd. Work bobble rib (working each rnd from *) for 3"/7.5cm. Bind off in rib.
Sew side and sleeve seams.

St st Cord

With dpn and F, cast on 3 sts. **Row 1 (RS)** K3, do not turn, slip sts to other end of needle; rep row 1 until cord measures approx 34"/86cm. Sew to outline of flower as indicated on chart.

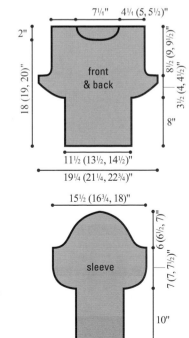

7¼"   4¼ (5, 5½)"
2"
18 (19, 20)"   front & back   8½ (9, 9½)"
3½ (4, 4½)"
8"
11½ (13½, 14½)"
19¼ (21¼, 22¾)"

15½ (16¾, 18)"
6 (6½, 7)"
sleeve   7 (7, 7½)"
10"
8¼ (9¼, 10¼)"

Attached Bobbles for Flower Center

(make 23)

With larger needles and D, cast on 1 st. K into front, back, front and back—4 sts. P4, turn, k4, turn, p4, turn, k2tog twice. Turn, p2 tog. Cut yarn leaving tail long enough to attach to center of flower as indicated in chart. Pull tails through to WS and tie.

CORDS
CIRCUS CIRCLE SCARF

KNITTED MEASUREMENTS

Approx 8"/20 cm x 42"/106.5cm including fringes

MATERIALS

• 6 1¾oz/50g balls (each approx 90yd/81m) of Tahki Yarns/Tahki•Stacy Charles, Inc. *Kerry* (alpaca/wool) in #5018 Orchid **4**
• One pair size 9 (5.5mm) needles OR SIZE TO OBTAIN GAUGE
• Size 7 (4.5mm) dpn
• Tapestry needle
• Stitch holder

GAUGE

16 sts and 20 rows = 4"/10cm over St st using size 9 (5.5mm) needles.
TAKE TIME TO CHECK GAUGE.

SCARF

Note Scarf is made in two pieces (beg with the fringe), which are grafted tog in center using Kitchener Stitch (see page 189).

Circles (make 14, 7 for each end of scarf) With dpn, invisibly cast on 5 sts (see page 188) and work 5-st St st cord (see page 188) for 5"/12.5cm. Graft ends tog. Set aside.

Staggered Circle Fringe

Using dpn, pick up 3 sts along one of the circles, work 4"/10cm of 3-st St st cord and leave on needle. Pick up 3 sts along next circle, work 2"/5cm of cord. Cont alternating 4" and 2"/10cm and 5cm fringe cords, until 7 fringes are made (last fringe cord is 4"/10cm). Leave 7 fringes on needle. Make 2nd set of 7 circle fringes and leave on separate needle. Slip 7 fringes to LH needle.
Single cast on 2 sts to RH needle, *k 3 cord sts from LH needle, cast on 4 sts; rep from *, end k 3 cord sts, cast on 2 sts—49 sts.
Row 1 (WS) P5, *k4, p3; rep from *, end p2.
Row 2 K2, *k1, slip 1, k1, p4; rep from * to last 5 sts, k1, slip 1, k3.
Rep rows 1 and 2 for 14"/35cm. Place sts on holder.
Slip rem fringes to LH needle and work as before for other end of scarf.

FINISHING

Graft two ends of scarf tog at center using Kitchener st. Fold 2-st side edges to WS and invisibly whip st down.

APPLIQUÉS
AMERICAN BEAUTY ROSE
CAPELET

SIZES

To fit Small (Medium, Large). Directions are for smaller size with larger sizes in parentheses. If there is only one figure, it applies to all sizes.

KNITTED MEASUREMENTS

Circumference at bottom 44 (49, 53)"/111.5 (124.5, 134.5)cm

Length 13 (14, 15)"/33 (35.5, 38)cm

MATERIALS

• 9 (10, 11) 1¾oz/50g balls (each 81yd/73m) of Tahki Yarns/Tahki•Stacy Charles, Inc. *Bunny* (merino/alpaca/acrylic) in #004 dusty rose mauve (A) **5**
• 1 .88oz/25g ball (each 269yd/245m) of Filatura Di Crosa/Tahki•Stacy Charles, Inc. *Baby Kid Extra* (super kid mohair/nylon) in #474 light mauve (B)
• One pair size 9 (5.5mm) needles OR SIZE TO OBTAIN GAUGE
• Tapestry needle
• One large hook and eye

GAUGE

15 sts and 24 rows = 4"/10cm over Basketweave st using Bunny and size 9 (5.5mm) needles.
TAKE TIME TO CHECK GAUGE.

STITCH GLOSSARY

S2kp2 (centered double decrease)
Slip 2 sts tog knitwise, k1, pass 2 slipped sts over.

Basketweave Stitch
(multiple of 4 sts plus 3)
Row 1 and all RS rows Knit.
Rows 2 and 4 *K3, p1; rep from * to last 3 sts, k3.
Rows 6 and 8 K1, *p1, k3; rep from * to last 2 sts, p1, k1.
Rep rows 1 to 8 for Basketweave st.

BACK

With A, cast on 83 (95, 103) sts. K 8 rows. Work 8 rows Basketweave st. Dec 1 st each side on next row, then every 4th row 14 (15, 16) times more—53 (63, 69) sts.

Shoulder shaping

Bind off 2 (2, 3) sts at beg of next 6 rows, 3 (4, 4) sts at beg of next 4 rows—29 (35, 35) sts. Bind off.

LEFT FRONT

Cast on 39 (43, 47) sts. Work same as back, working decs at side edge only (beg of RS rows), AT THE SAME TIME, when piece measures 12 (13, 14)"/30.5 (33, 35.5)cm from beg, end with a WS row and work as foll:

Neck shaping

Next row (RS) Bind off 5 (6, 6) sts (neck edge), work to end. Cont to bind off from neck edge 2 sts twice and 1 st 3 times. Cont shoulder shaping as for back.

RIGHT FRONT

Work to correspond to left front, reversing shaping.

FINISHING

Lightly block pieces. Sew side seams.

Front bands

With RS facing, pick up and k 37 (40, 43) sts along one front. K 3 rows. Bind off. Rep on other side.

Collar

With WS facing, pick up and k 75 (83, 83) sts evenly around neck. Work in Basketweave st beg with Row 2. Bind off 1 st at beg of next 8 rows—67 (75, 75) sts.

Next row (WS) (turning row) Knit.

Next row K5, [k2tog, k6 (7, 7)] 7 times, k2tog, k4 (5, 5)—59 (67, 67) sts.

Work 8 rows St st, inc 1 st each side every other row—67 (75, 75) sts.

Bind off loosely.

Whip st facing to neck edge.

American Beauty Rose (make 18)

With A, cast on 10 sts.

Row 1 (RS) Knit.

Row 2 and all WS rows Purl.

Row 3 K into front and back of every st—20 sts.

Row 5 K into front and back of every st—40 sts.

Row 7 K into front and back of every st—80 sts.

Join in 2 strands B, and using all 3 strands p 1 row. Bind off.

Twist rose into spiral and sew at back to hold spiral in place.

Sew 17 roses evenly around bottom edge of capelet and 1 at neck edge.

Garter Stitch Leaf (make 30)

Cast on 9 sts.

Rows 1, 3 and 5 (RS) K3, s2kp2, k3—7 sts.

Rows 2 and 4 K1, M1, k2, p1, k2, M1, k1—9 sts.

Row 6 K3, p1, k3.

Row 7 K2, s2kp2, k2—5 sts.

Row 8 K2, p1, k2.

Row 9 K1, s2kp2, k1—3 sts.

Row 10 K1, p1, k1.

Row 11 S2kp2—1 st. Fasten off.

Sew leaves randomly to bottom edge around roses. Sew 2 leaves to rose at neck edge.

Fringe

Holding 1 strand of A and 2 strands of B tog, cut 51 pieces 9"/23cm long. Using crochet hook, attach 3 lengths to bottom of each rose (see photo).

COLORS
FULLED BOLD FLORAL WRAP

KNITTED MEASUREMENTS

Approx 22" x 75"/55.75cm x 190.5cm before fulling

Approx 20" x 66"/50.5cm x 167.5cm after fulling

MATERIALS

• 7 1¾oz/50g balls (each approx 110yd/99m) of Trendsetter Yarns *Kashmir* (cashmere/silk) in #26809 plum (A) ④

• 4 balls #25385 tan (B)

• 2 balls each #29 burnt orange (C) and #27043 grape (D)

• 1 ball each #27018 olive (E), #25761 forest (F) and #25518 sky (G)

• One pair size 10 (6mm) needles OR SIZE TO OBTAIN GAUGE

• One size 10 (6mm) circular needle at least 29"/74cm long

• Corresponding beads (sample uses one package JC 997249 blue from Hirschberg Schultz & Co, Inc, Union, NJ, 07083)

• Sewing needle and thread to match

• Tapestry needle

GAUGE

17 sts and 24 rows = 4"/10cm over St st using size 10 (6mm) needles, before fulling. TAKE TIME TO CHECK GAUGE.

STITCH GLOSSARY

Inc row (RS) K2, yo, k to last 2 sts, yo, k2.

NOTES

Center of shawl is worked first, followed by mitered edgings on each end, then mitered side edgings. Flowers are worked in duplicate st after piece is knit. Beads are added after shawl is fulled.

SHAWL

Center

With A, cast on 64 sts and work in St st for 70"/177.5cm, ending with a WS row.

Top edge

Working Inc Row every RS row, work 3 rows in C, 19 rows in B, ending 2 rows C—88 sts. K 2 rows. Bind off knitwise from WS.

Lower edge

With RS facing and C, pick up and knit 64 sts along cast-on edge, working first inc on pick-up row. Complete as for top edge.

Side edges

With RS facing and C, use circular needle to pick up and k 276 sts along side edge working first inc on pick-up row. Complete as for top edge, ending with 300 sts.

FINISHING

Seam mitered corners.

Flowers Work duplicate stitch (see page 189) flowers following chart. **Top and bottom edges** Work one flower at center. **Side edges** Work 7 flowers along each side with 10 sts between each one and 4 sts on each end, not counting increase sts. Embroider leaf stems as on chart.

Fulling Wash in machine on hot, rinse in cold until fabric is fulled as desired. Sew 7 beads to each flower center. Line shawl (optional).

SIZES

To fit Small (Medium, Large). Directions are for smaller size with larger sizes in parentheses. If there is only one figure, it applies to all sizes.

KNITTED MEASUREMENTS

• Bust (closed) 46 (50, 54)"/117 (127, 137)cm

• Length 40½ (41½, 42½)"/103 (105.5, 108)cm

• Upper arm 15 (16¼, 17)"/38 (41, 43)cm

MATERIALS

• 15 (17, 18) 3½ oz/100g balls (each 93yd/85m) of Jaeger Handknits *Natural Fleece* (wool) in #523 Cowrie (MC) ⑤

• 3 (4, 4) balls #525 Peat (CC)

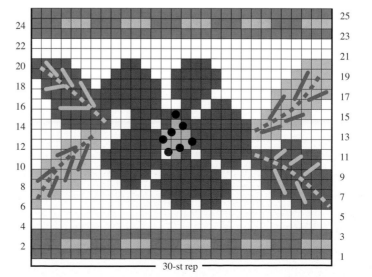

■ Plum (A)

□ Tan (B)

■ Burnt Orange (C)

▨ Olive (E)

■ Forest (F)

▨ Sky (G)

● Place Bead

▬ straight st with E

▬ straight st with F

▪▪▪▪ stem st with E

▪▪▪▪ stem st with F

30-st rep

- 6 1¾oz/50g balls (each 22yd/20m) of Jaeger Handknits *Fur* (kid/wool/polyamide) in #049 Antelope (A) 6
- One pair size 13 (9mm) OR SIZE TO OBTAIN GAUGE
- Stitch holders
- Bobbins (optional)
- Poly-fil

GAUGE

11 sts and 19 rows = 4"/10cm over garter stitch using size 13 (9mm) needles and Natural Fleece.
TAKE TIME TO CHECK GAUGE.

STITCH GLOSSARY

Double Loop Stitch

(multiple of 2 sts plus 1)
[The loops are formed on the RS but are worked on a WS row.]

Row 1 (WS) K1, *insert RH needle into next st as if to knit it, wind yarn over RH needle and around first and second fingers of left hand twice, then over RH needle point once more, draw all 3 loops through st and slip onto LH needle, insert RH needle through back of these 3 loops and original st and k them tog tbl, k1; rep from * to end.

Color and Loop Stitch Blocks

Work randomly placed Contrast Color and Loop Stitch Blocks according to the following principles:

- On RS, using bobbin of CC, work 10 to 13 sts in garter st. Work 6-row, (3-ridge) CC block over these sts. Work MC on either side of CC block using separate balls. Do not carry MC behind CC.
- Work only one block at a time along width of the fabric.
- Work 4 to 6 rows plain MC before beginning new CC block.
- Shift position of new block at least 9 sts to the left or right of previous block, so that the blocks are scattered on fabric.

- Every 4 or 5 blocks, work 6th row in Double Loop St.
- Every so often, work 5 to 6 Double Loops (over 11 to 13 sts) in MC.

BACK

With CC, cast on 40 (43, 46) sts. K 10 rows. With RS facing, cable cast on (see page 188) 34 (37, 40) sts—74 (80, 86) sts. K 10 rows. Change to MC and k 2 rows. Beg working randomly placed CC blocks (see notes), AT SAME TIME dec 1 st each side on next row then every 14th row 7 times more—58 (64, 70) sts. Work even until piece measures 28"/71cm above CC border (or desired length to underarm), ending with a WS row.

Armhole shaping

Bind off 4 (5, 6) sts at beg of next 2 rows. Dec 1 st each side every other row 3 (4, 4) times—44 (46, 50) sts. Work even until armholes measure 8½ (9¾, 10)"/21.5 (24.5, 25.5)cm.

Shoulder shaping

Bind off 4 sts at beg of next 2 rows, 4 (4, 5) sts at beg of next 4 rows. Place rem 20 (22, 22) sts on a holder for back neck.

Pockets (make 2)

With MC, cast on 14 sts. Work in St st for 6"/15cm. Cut yarn and place on holder.

LEFT FRONT

With CC, cast on 26 (28, 29) sts. K 10 rows. With RS facing, cable cast on 11 (12, 14) sts—37 (40, 43) sts. K 10 rows. Change to MC and k 2 rows. Beg working randomly placed CC blocks and loop sts and work decs at side edge as for back, AT SAME TIME, when piece measures 20½"/52cm above CC border, work as foll:

Pocket opening

Next row (RS) K9, bind off 14, k to end.
Next row K to bound-off sts, k14 sts of pocket from holder, k9.

Cont working CC blocks and side decs until piece measures same as back to armhole—29 (32, 35) sts. Work armhole shaping at side edge (beg of RS rows) as for back—22 (23, 25) sts. Work even until armhole measures same as back to shoulder.

Shoulder and neck shaping

Next row (RS) Bind off 4 sts, work to last 10 (11, 11) sts and place these sts on a holder for neck. Cont to bind off from shoulder edge 4 (4, 5) sts twice.

RIGHT FRONT

Work to correspond to Left Front, reversing all shaping and pocket placement.

SLEEVES

With CC, cast on 17 (19, 20) sts. K 10 rows. With RS facing, cable cast on 10 (12, 13) sts—27 (31, 33) sts. K 10 rows. Beg working randomly placed CC blocks and inc 1 st each side every 8th row 7 times—41 (45, 47) sts. Work even until sleeve measures 16 (16½, 17)"/40.5 (42, 43)cm above CC border, or desired length.

Cap shaping

Bind off 4 (5, 6) sts at beg of next 2 rows. Dec 1 st each side every other row 3 (4, 4) times—27 sts. K 12 (12, 14) rows. Dec 1 st each side every other row 7 times. Bind off 2 sts at beg of next 4 rows. Bind off rem 5 sts.

FINISHING

Sew shoulder seams.

HOOD

With WS facing, beg at left neck and using MC, slip 10 (11, 11) sts from left front holder on needle, pick up and k 7 sts along neck, slip 20 (22, 22) sts from back neck holder on needle, pick up 7 sts along right neck, slip 10 (11, 11) sts from right front holder to needle—54 (58, 58) sts. K 1 row, inc 8 (8, 10) sts evenly across—62 (66, 68) sts. Work even in garter st until hood measures 10"/25.5cm.

Last row K31 (33, 34). Fold hood in half, placing right sides tog with 31 (33, 34) sts on each needle. Work 3 needle joining (see page 188) across all sts.

Set in sleeves. Sew side sand sleeve seams. Whip stitch pocket lining to WS.

Fur balls (make 22)

Using A, cast on 4 sts.
Row 1 Knit into front and back of each st—8 sts.
Row 2 and all WS rows Purl.
Rows 3, 5 and 7 Knit.
Row 9 K2tog across row—4 sts.
Row 11 Pass 2nd, 3rd and 4th sts over first st.
Sew seam. Stuff with poly fil. Run tail through 4 cast-on sts, pull tightly and secure. Do not cut tail if hanging the ball. Attach 20 balls evenly spaced along bottom edge of coat alternating hanging position by 2"/5cm. Sew 1 fur ball to each front below hood.

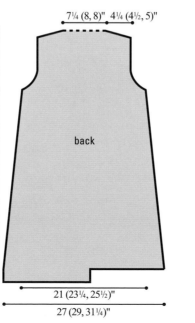

back

1¼"

8½ (9¾, 10)"

7¼ (8, 8)" 4¼ (4½, 5)"

30"

21 (23¼, 25½)"

27 (29, 31¼)"

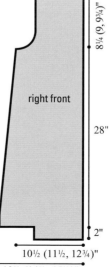

right front

1½"

8¼ (9, 9¾)"

28"

2"

10½ (11½, 12¾)"

13½ (14½, 15½)"

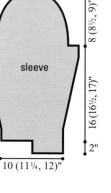

sleeve

15 (16¼, 17)"

8 (8½, 9)"

16 (16½, 17)"

2"

10 (11¼, 12)"

terms & abbreviations

3-needle joining technique Work sts of both layers tog, using 3-needle joining technique as foll: with RS of layers facing (top layer over bottom layer) and the needles parallel, insert a third needle into the first st on each needle and work them tog.

approx approximately

beg begin(ning)

bind off Used to finish an edge and keep stitches from unraveling. Lift the first stitch over the second, the second over the third, etc. (UK: cast off)

cable cast on Work same as **knit on cast on**, but after casting on 2 stitches, insert the right needle in between the first two stitches on the left needle, instead of into the first stitch.

cast on A foundation row of stitches placed on the needle in order to begin knitting.

CC contrast color

cm centimeter(s)

cn cable needle

cont continu(e)(ing)

dec decrease(ing)—Reduce the stitches in a row (knit 2 together).

dpn double pointed needle(s)

foll follow(s)(ing)

g gram(s)

garter stitch Knit every row. Circular knitting: knit one round, then purl one round.

inc increase(ing)—Add stitches in a row (knit into the front and back of a stitch).

invisible (invisibly) cast on Cut a strand of contrasting waste yarn approximately four times the required width. With the working yarn, make a slip knot and the needle. Hold the waste yarn beside the slip knot and *take the working yarn under it and over the needle from front to back. Bring the working yarn in front of the waste yarn. Keeping the waste yarn under the needle, repeat from the * until the required number of stitches is cast on. Remove the waste yarn only when the piece is finished.

k knit

k2tog knit 2 stitches together

knit on cast on Place a slip knot on left-hand needle, leaving a short tail. *Insert the right-hand needle knitwise into the stitch on left-hand needle. Wrap the yarn around the right-hand needle as if to knit. Draw yarn through the first stitch to make a new stitch, but do not drop the stitch from the left needle. Slip the new stitch to the left needle. Repeat from the * until the required number of stitches is cast on.

lp(s) loop(s)

LH left-hand

m meter(s)

M1 make one stitch—With the needle tip, lift the strand between last stitch worked and next stitch on the left-hand needle and knit into the back of it. One stitch has been added.

M1 p-st make one purl stitch—Work same as M1, but purl into back of strand.

make bobble Cast on 1 st. K in front, back, front, back and front again of st (5 sts made in one st). Turn. K 1 row, p 1 row, k 1 row. **Next Row** P2tog, p1, p2tog—3 sts. K 1 row. P3tog, fasten off.

MC main color

p purl

p2 (p3) (p5) tog purl 2 (3) (5) stitches together

pat pattern

pick up and knit (purl) Knit (or purl) into the loops along an edge.

pm place marker—Place or attach a loop of contrast yarn or purchased stitch marker as indicated.

rem remain(s)(ing)

rep repeat

rev St st reverse Stockinette stitch—Purl right-side rows, knit wrong-side rows. Circular knitting: purl all rounds. (UK: reverse stocking stitch)

rnd(s) round(s)

RH right-hand

RS right side(s)

sc single crochet (UK: dc - double crochet)

single cast on Place a slip knot on right-hand needle, leaving a short tail. Wrap yarn from ball around your left thumb from front to back and secure it in your palm with other fingers. Insert needle upwards through the strand on your thumb. Slip this loop from your thumb onto the needle, pulling the yarn from the ball to tighten it. Continue in this way until all the stitches are cast on.

S2KP Sl 2 sts tog, k1, pass the 2 sl sts over the k1—2 sts dec.

SKP Slip 1, knit 1, pass slip stitch over knit 1.

SK2P Slip 1, knit 2 together, pass slip stitch over k2tog.

sl slip—An unworked stitch made by passing a stitch from the left-hand to the right-hand needle as if to purl.

SP2P Sl 1 knitwise, p2tog, psso.

ssk slip, slip, knit—Slip next 2 stitches knitwise, one at a time, to right-hand needle. Insert tip of left-hand needle into fronts of these stitches from left to right. Knit them together. One stitch has been decreased.

ssp Slip 1, purl 1, pass slip stitch over purl 1.

st(s) stitch(es)

St st Stockinette stitch—Knit right-side rows, purl wrong-side rows. Circular knitting: knit all rounds. (UK: stocking stitch)

St st cord Cast on 3, 4, 5 or 6 stitches. Row 1 K3, 4, 5 or 6, do not turn, slide sts to other end of needle. Rep row 1 for desired length.

tbl through back of loop

tog together

WS wrong side(s)

wyib with yarn in back

wyif with yarn in front

work even Continue in pattern without increasing or decreasing. (UK: work straight)

yd yard(s)

yo yarn over—Make a new stitch by wrapping the yarn over the right-hand needle. (UK: yfwd, yon, yrn)

* Repeat directions following * as many times as indicated.

[ ] Repeat directions inside brackets as many times as indicated.

s t i t c h e s

kitchener stitch

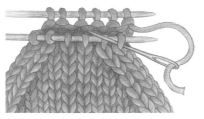

1 Insert tapestry needle purlwise (as shown) through first stitch on front needle. Pull yarn through, leaving that stitch on knitting needle.

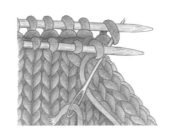

2 Insert tapestry needle knitwise (as shown) through first stitch on back needle. Pull yarn through, leaving stitch on knitting needle.

3 Insert tapestry needle knitwise through first stitch on front needle, slip stitch off needle and insert tapestry needle purlwise (as shown) through next stitch on front needle. Pull yarn through, leaving this stitch on needle.

4 Insert tapestry needle purlwise through first stitch on back needle. Slip stitch off needle and insert tapestry needle knitwise (as shown) through next stitch on back needle. Pull yarn through, leaving this stitch on needle.

Repeat steps 3 and 4 until all stitches on both front and back needles have been grafted. Fasten off and weave in end.

duplicate stitch

embroidery stitches

cross stitch

French Knot

straight stitch

stem stitch

acknowledgments

I am grateful to the staff of Sixth&Spring for their support on this book: Trisha Malcolm for her encouragement and faith in my creative ability, Carla Scott and Veronica Manno for their nonstop coordination skills, and especially Chi Ling Moy for her unyielding artistic talent and integrity.

Thanks to Eileen Curry, Nancy Henderson, Herris Stenzel, Dianne Weitzul, Joni Coniglio, Mary Lou Eastman, Sandy Prosser, Valerie Kurita, and Lisa Buccellato for the many hours they spent in helping me complete this major project.

Many thanks to Jack Deutsch and his staff—Eugene Mozgalevsky and Claudia Hehr—for their (as always) beautifully executed photography.

My gratitude to Diane Friedman and Stacy Charles of Tahki•Stacy Charles, Inc., for their generosity in supplying me with the beautiful yarn for the edgings and two of the designs. Thanks also to Jaeger, Classic Elite, and Trendsetter Yarns.

Thanks to my dear friends Jo Brandon, Emily Brenner, Wendy Chung, Chris Kitch, Leigh Merrifeld, and Jenni Stone.

Thanks to my readers and students for their ongoing support that continues to spark my creativity.

And finally…thanks to my husband Howard. You still got it, Mister!

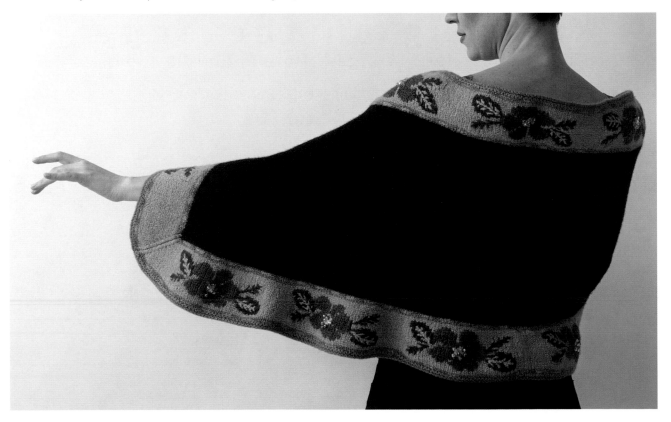

resources

United States Resources

Classic Elite Yarns
300 Jackson St., Bldg. #5
Lowell, MA 01852
classicelite@aol.com

Jaeger Handknits
4 Townsend West, Unit 8
Nashua, NH 03063

Tahki•Stacy Charles, Inc.
70-30 80th Street
Bldg. 36
Ridgewood, NY 11385

Tahki Yarns
distributed by
Tahki•Stacy Charles, Inc.

Trendsetter Yarns
16745 Saticoy Street #101
Van Nuys, CA 91406